This book will answer these questions

Should you try to build a business
for your invention or license it?

Where can you find potential licensees?

How do you get manufacturers to
want to license your product?

How do you handle it if you cannot
meet with potential licensees face-to-face?

How do you close the deal?

Why licensing was right for us
and may be right for you!

Mailbox Money!

A Step-by-Step Guide to Licensing your Invention for Royalties

Barbara Russell Pitts & Mary Russell Sarao

Successful Inventors, Speakers and Inventor Mentors

SECOND SIGHT PUBLISHING

First Edition

Cataloging in publication data:
Pitts, Barbara Russell, 1941 -
Sarao, Mary Russell, 1946 –
Mailbox Money! A Step-by-Step Guide to Licensing Your Invention for Royalties
p.cm

LCCN: 2012948525
ISBN: 978-0-9785222-7-8

Inventing – Handbooks, manuals, etc. 2. Inventing – Licensing. I. Title: Mailbox Money! A Step-by-Step Guide to Licensing your Invention for Royalties

This publication is designed to provide accurate and authoritative information with regard to the subject matter covered. It is sold with the understanding that the publisher is not engaged in rendering legal, accounting, or other professional advice. If legal advice or other expert assistance is required, the services of a competent professional person should be sought.

---From a Declaration of Principles jointly adopted by a Committee of the American Bar Association and a Committee of Publishers and Associations

Second Sight Publishing
Dallas, Texas
www.asktheinventors.com

DEDICATION

SINCE WE ESTABLISHED OUR WEBSITE IN 2001 WE have received hundreds of thousands of letters from novice inventors around the country and around the world. Some of the most common questions we have received are about licensing. Licensing seems to be an area in which the information available is confusing and vague. This book is for all those inventors! It was written as a step-by-step guide. It is meant to take all the mystery out of licensing; how to find potential licensees, how to contact them and how to get the best agreement possible.

ACKNOWLEDGEMENTS

THE INFORMATION AND KNOWLEDGE WE OFFER you in this book comes from years in the inventing business and hundreds of people who have generously and selflessly shared their experience and expertise with us. Whenever we have had a question that we could not answer, we have reached out to experts in that specific area of inventing and without fail they have provided the exact information we have needed to pass on to the inventors and would be inventors who write to us through our website, AsktheInventors.com. It would be impossible to list everyone without forgetting someone that should be mentioned so we will simply say, "Thank you!" to everyone who has helped us. You know who you are.

CONTENTS

INTRODUCTION xi

STEPS:

SHOULD I LICENSE MY INVENTION OR BUILD
A BUSINESS AROUND IT?..................................1

HOW CAN I FIND POTENTIAL LICENSEES? 21

EXACTLY HOW DO I PRESENT MY PRODUCT
FOR LICENSING? 43

WHAT HAPPENS IF I CANNOT MEET FACE-TO-
FACE WITH POTENTIAL LICENSEES? 95

CAN I NEGOTIATE THE LICENSE MYSELF? ...105

SUMMARY 111

ABOUT THE AUTHORS 117

PATENT & TRADEMARK DEPOSITORY LIBRARIES 121

INVENTOR CLUBS 129

INTRODUCTION

YOU HAVE A GREAT IDEA FOR A TERRIFIC NEW product and your first thought is. . . "I'll license it!" It sounds easy, right? Tell a company your great idea and they will do all the research, work and go to the expense of developing and marketing it. If only it were that easy!

It is not that easy, but it is not difficult either if you take it one step at a time. This book was written to help to guide you through those steps. We cannot be right there with you physically but through this book it will be as if we were right there with you. It will go into explicit details on how to prepare yourself to present your product for licensing, how to locate potential licensees, how to contact them and even what to say. It tells you how to get the help you need to get the best possible licensing agreement when it gets down to negotiating.

You may notice that we have used the masculine gender throughout the book. This is not meant to offend anyone or to suggest that all inventors and manufacturers are men. After all, the authors of this book are both women! It is simply done for ease of reading and to make the information less cumbersome for reading and therefore more understandable.

We also have constructed this book in question and answer form for two reasons. First, we are Ask the Inventors! Our life is all about answering questions that inventors ask. And second, we believe it makes it easier for the reader to quickly locate a particular section and find the information he needs without wading through a lot of stuff he doesn't want to read at that moment.

We want you to succeed and this book is our effort to give you all the information and tools you need to do just that.

Ready? Let's get started!

STEP ONE: THE DECISION

SHOULD I LICENSE MY INVENTION OR BUILD A BUSINESS AROUND IT?

ASSESSING YOUR SITUATION

How do I decide whether to license my invention or get it manufactured myself and build a business around it?

In order to determine if you should license your invention for royalty or build a business around it there are many factors to consider. The ultimate answer depends on your product and your situation. We will explore these factors below.

I already have a business with similar products. Should I license?

If you already own a business that is manufacturing and distributing other products and your new invention fits right into your line of products, it would make perfect sense to simply add your new invention to your existing line of products. You have the capability to handle the manufacturing yourself and you have the distribution and shipping logistics all figured out. You already have a business set up with all the attendant details in place. In this situation, adding your new invention to your existing line of products will only make your business stronger and make your entire line of products more attractive to retailers. Retailers love being able to buy multiple products in one category from one source.

I don't have a business now but I was thinking of starting one with my invention. Should I?

If you do not already have a business but want to spend full time building a business around your invention, that is a possibility but there are many obstacles to success that we will discuss in more detail. The dream of opening a business and the actual nuts and bolts of making it happen are two completely different things.

Do you want to spend full time on your product?

That would mean giving up your current job and waiting for the business to grow before it starts generating income to replace your current job.

Do you have the financial resources to start a new business?

A substantial amount of capital is required to even start.

Do you have the financial resources to keep the business afloat while it grows without causing undue stress on yourself and your family?

Conservatively, you would need enough capital to cover the business expenses and personal expenses for as much as one year.

Do you have a location from which to run your business?

Can you run it from your home? Would your city or town allow you to run it from your home? Many towns and cities have strict zoning laws that prohibit certain types of businesses from being operated in residential areas.

If your business would require you to rent or lease commercial property in order for customers to visit your business or store can you find a convenient location for reasonable rent?

Location! Location! Location! is the mantra we all hear regarding commercial property. Choosing the best commercial space for your business is challenging. Commercial properties can be quite expensive even if you are only leasing, but settling for a poor location can be even more costly in the long run. If your customers cannot find you and get to you easily it could cause your business to fail. Do not underestimate the value of a good location.

Would you need to rent storage or warehouse space to hold your product?

Your garage can only hold so much!

Are you ready to take on employees and all the attendant details that come along with having employees? What are those details?

Payroll

Any bookkeeper can tell you that payroll entails many things: matching taxes as well as federal and state quarterly reports to name just a few.

Income tax records and reports

Income tax records for both the federal government and often for state governments as well.

W-2 reports

1099 reports

Workers compensation reporting

Would your product be sold online?

If so, are you able to handle all of the shipping requirements yourself without it consuming all of your time?

Have you taken into consideration shipping costs?

The cost of shipping supplies and the cost of shipping your product, whether it will be the USPS, FedEX or UPS or a similar service must be figured into the cost of operating your business.

Might you need to hire a Fulfillment House?

Fulfillment houses can take care of receiving and filling orders but they will charge either by the item or a percentage of the sales. Can your business handle this extra cost?

Businesses have many bookkeeping requirements. Ask yourself these questions:

Are you able to handle Accounts Receivable and Accounts Payable yourself?

Are you able to close out your books each month and generate statements?

Are you able to make a Trial Balance?

Are you able to process credit card payments?

Are you able to prepare quarterly federal 941 reports?

Are you able to prepare annual 940 reports?

Are you able to file state sales tax reports?

If you aren't going to do these things yourself, can you hire someone to do them for you?

Legal expenses for a startup business can be substantial. What are some of those expenses?

Incorporation fees

DBAs (Business name, i.e. Doing Business As)

Trademarks

Patents

Attorney fees

What kind of insurance will be required?

Health insurance for employees

Property insurance for the business and

warehouse locations

Product Liability Insurance

Retailers require a substantial amount of product liability insurance on even the simplest products before they will order from you.

If your product requires an injection mold can you cover that expense?

Injection molds for even seemingly simple items can be costly, sometimes as much as $50-100K or more!

Can you buy the necessary equipment and facilities to manufacture your product? Can you cover the tooling up expenses?

Setting up the manufacturing equipment and the manufacturing facilities can be a major expense. Depending on what your product is, you may need all varieties of machines and equipment and the space in which to operate them efficiently.

Do you have the expertise to

design your own packaging?

Whole companies exist to research and design the most effective packaging for your product. Are you a graphic designer? If not, you may need to hire one. That is another expense that cannot be avoided.

Will you be able to travel to Asia from time to time if your product is outsourced there?

You will probably need to.

The Single Product Vendor Roadblock is real. Will you be able to challenge it?

What is the Single Product Vendor Roadblock?

Retailers universally do not want to deal with a vendor who has only one product to sell to them. Their buyers have limited time to allow to vendors and their representatives who bring products for their consideration. It is almost impossible for someone with only one product to even get an appointment with the buyers for these retailers. Some single product vendors engage product representatives who take many products in the same category (office supplies, electronics, etc.) to add their product to the line that they are showing, but this involves a percentage of the profit going to the product rep.

Another problem faced by single product vendors is the fact that every inch of shelf space in the stores is already allotted to the representatives who bring products to them. It is far easier to get some of that coveted shelf space by getting in the door with a vendor who already has shelf space in those stores. They can replace one of their lesser selling items with your new item. This is one of the big reasons why many people prefer to license their inventions because the manufacturers already have shelf space in the very stores in which they want to see their products selling.

What about the shopping channels, such as HSN or QVC? Could I run my business that way and avoid many of the above-mentioned problems?

You could. The main things you need to consider if you are thinking of marketing in that way are:

You will have to have the money and ability to get the product manufactured and shipped to the shopping channels.

You are at the mercy of those channels regarding when and how much product they want to order.

If your product doesn't sell well they have the option of sending it back to you so you would need to have a backup plan of where you would take it at that point.

If your product is selected for televising, there is no guarantee that they will continue to order from you on a regular basis.

But, if you present your product on a shopping network it does get immediate wide attention and that could be a springboard for getting a license agreement because you can point to the sales numbers to prove that there is a market for your product.

What about infomercials? That would be like my own shopping channel and would afford me more control, wouldn't it?

It certainly could if you have enough capital to get an infomercial made and to buy the airtime on one or more networks. There are a few (very few) legitimate places that will put the money into making the infomercial and airing it. They are extremely selective about which products they will take on since they are risking their own capital but there have been some big successes with this method. One such company, located in Dallas, Texas is Exceptional Products, http://www.sellontv.com/default.aspx.

This is another method for getting immediate wide distribution and proving a market for your product, thereby paving the way to licensing.

We are sure that there are other such companies but we don't personally know any of them. There are many links on the Internet offering this kind of opportunity but some of them are sure to be scammers so if you elect to look into this marketing method be sure to thoroughly check out anyone that you are considering working with.

What if my patent gets infringed?

If you have a great product you can be sure that you will be infringed. As an independent product developer do you have the financial resources to enforce your patent? Patent infringement lawsuits are expensive, sometimes costing $1,000,000 or more! Do you have a war chest of money set aside for this eventuality?

Factors to consider if you are thinking of licensing your product: Are you willing to turn over the manufacturing and marketing to someone else?

Once your product is licensed, it is essentially out of your hands. Your license agreement will spell out any rights that you still have regarding your patent but generally, your rights relate to quality control, the right to see new products under your license agreement before they are marketed and rights related to your royalty payments. Your licensee will be making and distributing your product and you will probably have no say in how that is accomplished.

Are you willing to locate a licensee and work out a deal?

While there are many advertisements stating that others are willing to take on the marketing of your patent for a license agreement, there are almost none who are ethical. Your chances for licensing success are far better if you do this yourself and this book will teach you how to do that.

Do you want to be free to pursue other interests?

If you are working full time running your business you are not likely to have a great deal of free time, at least for the first year or so and perhaps even longer if your business requires a lot of your attention. Many who elect to license their inventions do so because they don't want to be tied down with the day-to-day tasks involved. Creative people often want to keep their time available for pursuing other new products or related activities. And some who have successfully licensed their inventions have done so because they just want to do what they want when they want . . . sometimes nothing at all. They do so because they want the freedom to spend their time as they choose.

Do you want immediate wide distribution?

We have already discussed the Single Product Vendor Roadblock. It is almost impossible for someone with only one product to get immediate wide distribution without licensing unless he creates and airs a successful infomercial, which can be very expensive, or is immediately very successful on one of the shopping channels, such as HSN or QVC. We will discuss these options in more detail later in this book.

Would you like to avoid the costs of infringement lawsuits?

We briefly mentioned infringement lawsuits and how enforcing one's patent can often cost a million dollars or more. If you license your patent exclusively to one company you can have it written into your license agreement that they will be responsible for patent enforcement in the event of infringement.

Should I license exclusively to one manufacturer or non-exclusively to multiple manufacturers?

For most independent inventors exclusive licensing makes a lot more sense than non-exclusive licensing for the following reasons:

It is difficult to get manufacturers to agree to a non-exclusive license unless you have a brand name that the public already wants to buy, such as Disney or NASCAR. For brand new products, the manufacturer will want the advantage in the marketplace that an exclusive agreement will afford him.

If you license non-exclusively you are responsible for enforcing your patent, a very expensive prospect.

It is possible to license your product exclusively to more than one manufacturer if those manufacturers cater to different markets. For example, if you have a product that is primarily sold to general retail and there is another manufacturer who provides product to a specific market sector other than retail such as the medical industry for example, you may be able to license exclusively to both but only because they would not both be selling to the same customers.

If I license my invention, how much royalty can I expect?

The general rule of thumb is that the average exclusive license royalty is around 5%, but it can vary due to a number of factors. Sometimes a mid-sized company will pay a higher percentage of royalty, usually from 5% to 7%, depending on how popular the product will be, and if there is a great enough difference between the manufacturing cost and selling price. Larger companies will often pay 2% to 4% but they will have a larger distribution channel, making up the difference for the inventor. Sometimes larger companies will fashion royalties on a sliding scale based on the projected life and popularity of a product. Bottom line . . . your royalty will be what you can negotiate.

Is it important to have a trademarked name for my product?

It sure was for us! We came up with the name Ghostline® for our poster board product because we thought it was descriptive and catchy. We filed for and received a trademark. It was only after we were granted the federally registered trademark that we were told that poster board was a commodity and it is not customary to get trademarks for commodity products. It was a blessing that we didn't know that beforehand because when our license agreement was negotiated the licensee liked the name so much that the trademark, Ghostline® was included as a part of the agreement.

You may be asking yourself, "Why was that important?" Because patents have a limited lifetime after which they expire. Trademarks never expire so long as they are in continuous use. Our license agreement states that when the patent expires the licensee will continue to pay us royalties (at a reduced rate) as long as they continue to use our trademark. Our hope is that by the time the patent expires our licensee will have spent so much time, money and effort in promoting the trademark that they will not want to give it up. The trademark will have built up an equity value in the marketplace that would be foolish to squander.

STEP TWO: LOCATING A LICENSEE

HOW DO YOU FIND
POTENTIAL LICENSEES?

How do I locate companies who might license my invention?

Have you looked at similar products?

If not, that is the first place to look! Go to any store that might have products in the same general category of products as your invention. On the packaging you will see the name of the manufacturer, where they are located and many times you will find a website as well. Any manufacturers that make products in the same category as your product are potential licensees since they already have a market presence in that category and distribution channels in place.

Have you done an Internet search for similar products?

Many times you can find products on the Internet that you cannot find anywhere else. Those products may be great sellers, however, so you must not discount Internet companies as potential licensees. Just go to your favorite search engine (try Google.com/products) and type in a one or two word description of your product. Then start exploring those links. Some of the companies you find will be companies with which you are already familiar from looking at the same category of products in stores. A few will probably be new. Take note of those. Learn whatever you can about the companies; where they are located, telephone numbers, contact information, etc.

Have you checked the business section of your library?

If you haven't then run, don't walk, to your closest main library! The business section of your main library holds a wealth of information, much of it that is not available online. They have business databases such as ReferenceUSA, Hoovers, Dun & Bradstreet's Million Dollar Companies and several more. These databases, that may be accessible through your home computer, will provide a wealth of information about potential licensees. You can find out who the biggest players are in the market you hope to tap. You can find out annual sales (sometimes broken down into categories), numbers of employees, key personnel and often even their contact numbers and e-mail addresses.

Also in the business section of your local main library you will find a gold mine of information in the trade directories. So far as we know these directories (they are massive) are only available in the libraries. They list every US manufacturer in a specific category. For example, when we were looking for poster board manufacturers we were directed to the Lockhart-Post Directory of the Pulp and Paper Industries. We never knew such a thing existed but it was incredible. It lists every manufacturer in the US that makes anything made of paper.

We were able to quickly identify all the companies that manufactured poster board. It told us the percentage of their sales that consisted of poster board and even how much were domestic sales and how much were international.

It told us if the companies were publicly or privately owned, where they are located and information on how to contact key personnel.

You must consult these directories! You may find companies that are huge in your market that you were completely unaware of because they have many subsidiaries operating under unfamiliar names. Your reference librarians can be an invaluable help because they are familiar with every resource that is available.

Also, in the back of some of these directories you will find a list of distributors. These are sales people who distribute products for many different manufacturers. If you are making and distributing your invention on your own while you wait for your patent to issue, these distributors can make an enormous difference in the coverage and volume of your distribution. A good distributor can increase your income dramatically. They usually work within specific sectors of the market (for example, school supplies, etc.) and also within specified geographic boundaries. In order to get nationwide coverage you may wish to engage the services of multiple distributors.

What is the Thomas Register and how can it help me?

The Thomas Register (www.thomasnet. com) is a list of US manufacturers organized by products, key words, and geographic area. In the library it is a set of 20 volumes in the reference section. The Thomas Register in the library offers more complete listings than the online Thomas Register but the online version seems quite comprehensive to us. Manufacturers must join the Thomas Register in order to be listed so it may not include every single manufacturer.

Another benefit of the online Thomas Register is that it has direct links to the websites of the various manufacturers. This can be a real time saver!

Is it possible to find potential licensees on the USPTO website?

You can! They don't have any sort of list but you may be able to find exactly what you are looking for in a creative way.

Look on your patent or your patent application. It will list the classifications into which your invention falls. Go to www.uspto.gov as if you were searching for patents except this time choose classification number as the search criteria. It will bring up every single invention that is in that classification. Begin paging through them looking for assignees.

Some of the assignees will be companies for whom the inventors work. Others may be companies that have licensed products from independent inventors. Those are the ones you are seeking. Any company that a patent has been assigned to may be a potential licensee. Write down the company name then go to your favorite search engine and look them up. You may find companies that you would otherwise never find in this somewhat convoluted way. But, it can work, so who cares, right?

Where are the assignees shown on the patents?

Look on the front page of the patent and right under the abstract (short summary of the invention near the top of the page), you will find the listing of the inventor or inventors. Immediately under that line, if the patent has been assigned, you will find the assignee.

Are there tricks to refining the search on the patent database?

There certainly are and we know a man who is an expert at using the USPTO database information to his advantage.

George Burkhardt is a San Antonio, Texas

inventor who is known for his ingenuity in locating and contacting potential licensees and for his success with his methods. He has developed a method for using the USPTO database that brings the inventor right to the individuals who may be able to assist in providing entry into the right office at the chosen manufacturer. Here is how he does this: Being aware that large manufacturers have employees who invent in-house products that are assigned to the company as part of their employment contracts, he decided to locate a former company inventor who could provide him with senior management contacts or referrals.

George wanted to obtain a senior level contact person at XYZ Manufacturing (fictitious name). He did a quick patent search on the USPTO website in which he put "XYZ Manufacturing" in the "term" box and he selected "assignee" in the "fields" box. This produced a list of patents in which XYZ Manufacturing was the assignee. He knew the states in which XYZ had facilities and he looked for inventors on the front page of the patents that lived in different states. His thought here was that a person who lived in a different state no longer worked for XYZ and would be a good contact. He made a couple of phone calls and found a former XYZ engineer who had previously invented a tool for the company. This man provided George with contacts for XYZ and also for another company where some of his former co-workers had relocated to senior management. These were the exact contacts he needed! Within weeks George had a proposed license agreement. You will learn the outcome of George's great "detective work" in locating the right people in the next step.

This is also a way to find independent inventors who may never have worked for the company but still licensed a patent to them. These people will also know the names and contact information for the key players to contact regarding licensing.

Will a website for my product

help me to find a licensee?

The answer is yes and no. If you create a website for your product hoping that a potential licensee will see it and contact you just dying to license your product. . . the answer is probably no. The Internet is massive. Chances of a potential licensee just stumbling across your website are next to zero.

A website for your product, however, can help you to find a licensee. You can use it as an online brochure for your product. It can show your product, explain all its benefits and even have a video demonstration. When contacting potential licensees it is great to be able to point them to your website and hopefully create enough interest to get them to call you about potential licensing.

Warning: A website does not take the place of a face-to face meeting or a written presentation! It is simply an enhancement of the entire package.

Are there other creative ways

to find licensees?

There are as many ways as there are creative people! We have heard of some who wrote press releases and managed to get them into newspapers and magazines. This certainly gets your product before a lot of people.

We don't know of success stories using this method but there may be some. One thing is certain…getting more publicity can only enhance your chances that the right person will see your product. And as Jeff Crilley, former Fox newsman and author of the bestselling, Free Publicity, says, any time someone else writes about you or your product, there is so much more credibility in the public eye because they know that in paid advertising, you paid for the good things to be said. Even though press releases come directly from the source of the product, we believe they are more credible to the reader because they are included as a public announcement rather than as a paid advertisement.

In the same vein, many people, inventors

and others, are getting a lot of attention by using social media, such as Facebook, Twitter, LinkedIn, Ryze, and YouTube. This is something that costs little or nothing to do and could create a buzz for your new product.

The trick here is to find a way to drive people to view the website. Nick Romer, author of the bestselling, Make Millions Selling on QVC, says that if you can create something slightly outrageous, such as the man with the blender company who famously ground up his iPhone to a powder to prove the strength of the blender, you may get very popular very quickly.

Renee C. Quinn is an expert on social media and how to use it to advantage. Check out this website for her excellent articles on how to use social media, http://www.ipwatchdog.com/about/gene-patent-attorney/.

Where is the best place to find potential licensees?

Tradeshows! We saved the best for last.

Tradeshows are the absolute best place to find potential licensees. If you go to the tradeshow for your category of product you may find dozens of potential licensees all under one roof!

You are undoubtedly wondering how to locate the tradeshow for your product. It's simple. For example, if your product is a golf product you will want to go to a golf tradeshow. Put golf tradeshow into any search engine and it will pop up with a list of upcoming golf tradeshows. Many industries have multiple tradeshows. The golf industry for example has at least 20 shows coming up in the next year.

Most categories of products do not have that many shows but it is not unusual for a specific category of products to have 3-5 shows per year.

How do I get into a tradeshow?
Aren't they for industry insiders?

You are not a manufacturer or a retailer, right? How do you get in? You join as an associate member! Joining as an associate member costs much less than joining as a regular member. Regular memberships may cost $1-2 thousand dollars but associate memberships usually cost only a few hundred dollars. Product developers are entitled to join as associate members. Then, you will be an insider!

What does my associate membership get me?

It gets you credentials to be there. It gives you the freedom to walk the show and speak to anyone there. You are officially an industry insider! You are supposed to be there and you will be treated as someone who belongs there.

It gets you an association directory! This is big! The industry directories list all the members, the products they sell and the contact information for key individuals in each company.

In addition to getting a directory for your use when the next directory comes out you will be listed as an associate member giving you even more credibility and insider status.

Should I rent a booth?

No, you are not there to sell product. You are there to identify potential licensees. Do not take your prototype or written presentation to the tradeshow.

Why shouldn't I take my prototype and written presentation to show them at the tradeshow?

Giving away all of your information at the tradeshow gives them a chance to turn it down without really considering it. At this point in the show they are tired and they may not be the only decision-maker on new products. If, on the other hand, you just pique their interest and exchange business cards with them, you will have a chance to get that sit-down appointment where you can really showcase your new product.

What should I do at the tradeshow?

Most tradeshows are 2-4 days in length. During the first few days of the show your job is to simply walk the floor. Look at each and every booth. When you look at each booth ask yourself if your product would fit right in with their product line. If it would, make note of that booth, the booth number and the company name. Do not attempt to speak to anyone during the first few days of the show.

The manufacturers who have the booths are selling to their retail accounts and do not want to be distracted by anything else. If you were to try to speak to them at this time they would be annoyed and may not give you the time of day later when they will have time to talk to you.

Wait until the last day of the show to begin approaching the booths of the potential licensees you have identified. On the last day of the show they are happy to speak with you. Their selling is done and they are just passing the time waiting to be able to take down their booth and go home.

Approach them with a big smile, handshake and eye contact. Give them your business card and identify yourself as a product developer who has a product that would fit right in with their product line. Ask them if they ever license products from independent product developers. They will give you one of three answers. They may say, "No, we do everything in-house." If that is the case thank them for their time and move on to your next potential licensee.

Or they may say, "We haven't, but we might." Or, "Sure, we do that from time to time." Bingo! These are the folks you want to talk to. Do not describe your invention in detail; rather, tell them the problem that it solves. If they press you further tell them that you would like to sit down in person to show it to them in a few weeks. Explain that you will not take up much of their time but you believe the product is so unique and perfect for their company that it would warrant a short appointment.

Take their business card and tell them that you will call for an appointment in a week or so.

Should I join the trade association even if I cannot go to the tradeshow?

Absolutely! Joining as an associate member

gives you credibility within the industry. Potential licensees are much more likely to give you an appointment to show your product if you can tell them that you are a member of their trade association. It is almost like saying you belong to their club. Credibility and trust that you are professional and know what you are doing is immediately established.

Shouldn't I protect my invention before I begin showing it for licensing? I can't afford the time or money for a patent.

If your product is not already patented or patent pending, you will need to take action to protect it before showing it for licensing. Most manufacturers will not consider or even look at a product that is not protected because it would make no sense for them to pay you for something that they could make and sell without paying you. It also does not make financial sense for them to pay you for something that their competitors can just make and sell without paying anyone.

So, what is an independent inventor to do?

Provisional Patent Application to the rescue! A Provisional Patent Application (PPA) will make a product immediately patent pending for a full year. It costs only $125 at this writing to file a PPA and the format is much looser than it is for filing for a regular utility patent. Basically a PPA will "hold your place in line" at the patent office by allowing you the earliest filing date possible and allowing you to describe your product as patent pending. The PPA itself will never result in an actual patent. But, from the moment you file your PPA, whether you file online or drop it into the mailbox, your invention will be legally patent pending.

Within one year after you file your Provisional Patent Application (PPA), you must file for a utility patent or lose the advantage of the earlier filing date. Provisional Patent Applications are not even looked at by the examiners at the patent office until they are referred to in your Utility Patent Application.

Another advantage of the PPA is that you can include multiple invention ideas in one PPA. It is always best to include every possible detail (including all possible applications) for each invention included in your PPA.

Provisional Patent Applications are very attractive to independent inventors because they allow the inventors to have as early a filing date as possible and it allows them to list their product as patent pending. That gives the inventor one year in which to find a licensee without going to the expense of filing for a utility patent. For inventors who wish to build a business around their invention it gives them one year in which to test the viability of their product.

If the inventor is successful in finding a licensee during the one-year PPA period then he can have it written into the license agreement that the licensee would be responsible for all the costs of filing for and maintaining the regular utility patent but the inventor would still be listed as the owner of the patent.

Rates vary widely for writing Provisional Patent Applications. Most attorneys and patent agents charge $800-$2,400 to write the provisional patent application.

Writing a Provisional Patent Application is something that an independent inventor can do himself with the help of the book Patent Pending in 24 Hours by Pressman and Stim. This book leads you through the process step-by-step.

Provisional Patent Applications are not available to those filing Design Patent Applications.

If you want to find a patent professional, attorney or agent, in your area and are seeking good assistance for the lowest possible fees, here's a tip from our friend, George Burkhardt. Going into the USPTO database, https://oedci.uspto.gov/OEDCI/, select your geographic region and search for patent agents and attorneys that have a residential address. These agents/attorneys are often retired or work at home and will likely be less expensive than those that work in a business district.

If you decide to go ahead and file a Utility Patent Application, and some independent inventors do, you will definitely need to get professional help with the writing and filing of your patent. This will be very important to you when it comes to licensing because manufacturers will want as airtight a patent as possible. Their attorneys will look over your patent with a fine-toothed comb to be certain that they would be protected from competition if they licensed with you. They will also look it over to see if there is any way that they could circumvent your patent with one of their own and make a similar product! If they like your product well enough to consider licensing, you can be sure that they will also consider how they could get around your patent and manufacturer the product without having to license.

STEP THREE: MAKING CONTACT

HOW DO I PRESENT MY PRODUCT FOR LICENSING?

I'm so nervous about calling a potential licensee! Is there some secret protocol, certain words or phrases I need to use in order to appear professional and to get to the right person? And, how do I know who the right person is?

There are no secret words or phrases to use with the receptionist but we will give you a few tips that may be helpful. If you have located your licensing target at a trade show, chances are that you will have his business card and a number for a phone that will ring right on his desk, circumventing the receptionist altogether.

If you have not been to a trade show but you have researched the company you should have names and titles of one or more of the people you want to reach. Simply ask the receptionist to put you through to these individuals by name. If you reach one of those robot receptionists in the form of a recorded message asking you to select numbers to reach different individuals, we recommend that you listen to the options until they tell you which option will get you an operator. Then ask that person to connect you to the individual whose name you have found in your research.

If they tell you that the person you are requesting is no longer there (This happens more often than you would think; apparently there is a lot of turnover in these large companies.), ask for the product manager of the particular category of your product, or the vice president of marketing or the vice president of sales. If you get resistance, just tell them that you have a new product you would like to discuss with an executive of the company in regard to licensing.

If you are calling a large company you will need to try one of the above methods to reach the right person. If you are calling a mid-sized company, ask for the president by name. You may just reach him! If you don't you'll reach someone in his office and they will direct you to the right person when you explain the reason for your call. And, when a call is routed from the president's office you can bet that whoever gets the call will respond to it.

I didn't make it to a trade show. How do I handle the call once I have reached someone?

Okay. Say you have reached someone in the new products division of a larger company or the president of a smaller company. The first thing you will do is introduce yourself.

One big mistake many new inventors make at this point is to introduce themselves as inventors. Huh? An inventor introducing himself as an inventor is a mistake? Yes, and here's why. While we certainly are inventors and we call ourselves that among ourselves, the word inventor sometimes has a negative connotation to others. When they hear the word inventor they may think of someone tinkering in their garage or, even worse, someone like Doc from the movie Back to the Future! It sounds much more professional to introduce yourself as a Product Developer. That is also what you are.

The goal here is to get their attention with that first phone call so that you can develop a relationship with them and be taken seriously by them. It will also boost your credibility greatly if you have a company name to use along with your name. We aren't suggesting that you lie if you don't have a company name to use, but it is a simple matter to create a company for yourself so that it doesn't sound like it's just you alone with your product.

Do I need to set up a business just to go to trade shows and present my product?

You don't have to, but there is a shortcut that would allow you to do just that with very little effort and money. Here's what you can do:

Select a name for your business. Ideally, it should be a general sounding name that is not tied to one product. While we believe that the name you choose for your product should be descriptive of the product, we think it's better to name your company something that doesn't indicate anything. In this way you can place everything you do under the umbrella of the same company name. In other words, instead of calling your company The Super Duper Sink Drain Company, you could call it General Products Company. You might want to select two or three possible names for your company to save you some trouble in case your first choice is not available.

Go to the County Clerk's office in your city and apply for a DBA (Doing Business As).

In most cities this will cost around $11.00 and they will issue you a certificate in your company name right then. You can technically consider yourself in business at this point if you are only going to use the DBA for printing business cards and presenting your product. If you already have a business bank account you can add that DBA to your existing account. Otherwise, you don't even have to have a bank account at this juncture.

You can now take that business name and print up business cards. This gives you an extra level of credibility with prospective licensees. Some people have been known to just keep a DBA for years in order to have a company name. Only you know that your business is just a name! When you get a license agreement you have time to turn your company name into an LLC or a corporation. Just one little caveat here: The DBA you have obtained will only be legal in the county in which you obtained it.

If you eventually decide to incorporate you will probably need to obtain the DBA in every county in your state. You can do this by contacting the Secretary of State's office in your state capitol. There is a special area dedicated to DBAs in these offices. You can probably handle it with a phone call and a credit card. If, when you decide to do that, you find that the name is not available everywhere that you need it, you can always start over with a different name. It would only involve obtaining a new DBA at that time.

Once you have introduced yourself by your name and your company name (if you have one) and identified yourself as a product developer you have set the stage. If you have mentioned a company name remember to refer to yourself as "we" rather than "I". You will have more credibility if they believe that there is a company behind you than if you approach them as an individual.

It is important to remember here that the next thing you say at this point should have as much impact as possible because they don't know you and they may not have a lot of interest in what you have to say unless it is something that will benefit them. So your next statement should be something to excite them. What will excite them? Something that will make money for their company! A new product that fits right into their existing line can often re-energize their brand and bring new customers. Sometimes it can even get the manufacturer into retail chains that they were previously unable to get their products into because they didn't have anything to offer that their competitors didn't also offer. The retailer will want the product that they can only get from this manufacturer.

So, what should that statement be? We will print below a sample script for that telephone conversation.

Product Developer: *Hello, Mr. Jones! This is Jane Doe and I'm with Great Creations. We're product developers based in Tulsa, Oklahoma. We have a brand new patented (or patent pending) product that is a perfect match for your line of products. We're looking to license it exclusively to one manufacturer and we want to show it to you first.*

(In this opening statement you have identified yourself as a professional, told him where you are calling from, and told him you have a wonderful new protected product that is available for exclusive licensing.)

Mr. Jones: *You have? What is it?*

Product Developer: *It's a simple way of solving a problem common to dog walkers. It's so perfect for your product line that we would like to bring it and show it to you. When could we do that?*

(Here, you have told him the problem that your invention solves, shown enthusiasm, and asked for the appointment.)

Mr. Jones: *Just tell me what it is.*

Product Developer: *It's an improved leash that solves the problem of walking more than one dog at the same time. I know you are aware of the problems inherent in the leashes that are designed for this purpose. This leash easily and inexpensively makes those other products obsolete. I would really like the opportunity to show you how it works and I'll gladly travel to your location for just a few minutes of your time.*

(Here, you have given him a bit more information about your invention without revealing how it accomplishes the goal, acknowledged that he is an expert in his field, listed the main benefits and made it easy for him to give you the appointment.)

If he says that he is unaware of the problems with similar products, explain briefly the problem that is happening with the current products that your new product solves. Then, try to nail down the appointment without giving him any more specifics.

What if he insists on knowing what it is?

It's not really necessary to be secretive but you may generate more interest and get to schedule the in-person meeting if you don't give him too much detail on the phone call. The purpose of this call is to pique his interest enough to get the appointment. If he insists, don't anger him;

go ahead and tell him what it is so he will see that it truly is a logical extension to his product line. If you tell him exactly what it is right at the beginning of the conversation it gives him the opportunity to cut you off with something like, "We already carry enough pet leashes", when with a little finesse you may get right in for that coveted appointment. The main thing to remember here is to always be someone that he would like to meet with. Be friendly and courteous.

When should I give them my written presentation?

If you can get the face-to-face meeting, that is best. If you are able to meet with them personally, don't give them your printed presentation until you are finished with your oral presentation. You don't want them looking through the presentation while you are talking. You want their full attention so that they can see your facial expressions and your passion for the invention. The written presentation is designed to speak on your behalf after you have left or if you are unable to meet with them in person.

If I cannot get a face-to-face meeting or cannot travel to the manufacturer's location, is the written presentation the only thing I should send them?

No. Send a prototype if you have one that you can send, once you have made contact with someone there and created some kind of relationship, so that he knows your package is coming and he is expecting it. Also, and this is especially important, send a great, professional-looking sell sheet. While the written presentation will explain in some detail why the manufacturer should add the product to his line of products, the sell sheet will be the thing that creates in him the desire to read over the presentation.

Busy executives usually limit the amount of time they will allow for looking at something new unless there is something about it that grabs their attention. This is the function of the sell sheet. The sell sheet is like a tiny billboard, trumpeting the benefits of this new product. The sell sheet should have some photos or some type of graphics along with a list of the benefits of the product. It could include a link to a video on YouTube demonstrating your product, if you have one. Stephen Key, author of, One Simple Idea, has written eloquently about sell sheets. You can see some samples of powerful sell sheets on his website at, http://stephenkey.com/2011/04/13/sell-sheet-samples/.

I went to the tradeshow and picked up business cards. How do I approach the phone call?

If you have met them at a trade show it is usually much easier to get the appointment and they don't insist on knowing exactly what you have. Remember in step two that we said that being an associate member of their organization makes you an insider? It's very true. If you have left your business card when you visited with them at the trade show, they probably scanned it into their computer and will be able to easily pull up your card on their screen. Even if they don't have your card, just mentioning that you met them at the trade show tells them that you are one of them and you will have their ear.

When calling someone whom you met at a trade show the conversation may go something like this:

Product Developer: *Hello, Mr. Jones. I'm John Doe with Creative Products out of Tulsa, Oklahoma. We're product developers. I met you at the XYZ tradeshow last month. I know you met a lot of people so I don't expect you to remember me.*

(At this point he may ask if you gave him a business card and he will then pull it up on his computer.) You have established that you are a member of his trade organization and this gives you tremendous credibility as a product developer so you don't have to go through all the explanations that were necessary in the earlier conversation when the product developer has no tie to the manufacturer.

Product Developer continues: *We visited right*

at the end of the trade show about the fact that we have a new patented (or patent pending) product that fits right into your line of products. We're looking to license it exclusively and we'd love to show it to you.

Mr. Jones: *Sure! Can you tell me the general category of the product so I can get the right people in to the meeting?*

Product Developer: *Sure thing! It's an improved pet leash.*

Mr. Jones: *Got it! How soon would you like to come?*

At this point you simply set the appointment. It really is that easy when you are a member of their trade association.

The above methods are based on cold-calling, although the second one, having joined the trade association, is far less of a cold call than the first. There is another method, developed by a very creative San Antonio inventor. Remember George Burkhardt, the inventor in the previous chapter who developed a method for locating the right senior level people with his target manufacturers? Here's another of his simple but very effective methods and has resulted in a very lucrative licensing agreement for the tool he developed. George calls this a type of "pull-through" marketing. It doesn't involve going to a tradeshow or even joining a trade association, although that is still a good idea. Follow along closely because this is pure genius!

George knew that he wanted to license his tool, the Drain Plug Pro™, to a large manufacturer of similar tools. He first went to auto parts stores looking for manufacturers that made similar tools. Armed with a list of manufacturers of similar tools, he then went back to his computer and to the online database of his library. There, in ReferenceUSA, he input the manufacturers he had obtained at the auto parts stores. The information in that database allowed him to determine which manufacturers of tools in the same category as his were the largest. He identified three large companies.

George knew that most large retailers had product managers who managed their tool products. He also knew that the tool manufacturers had product managers as well. He felt that if he could approach the product manager at the retailer, he could get contact information and a referral to the corresponding product manager at the manufacturer. Here, we will disguise the names of the manufacturers and brands but you will understand the concept. He wanted to reach ABC Manufacturing Company. He knew that DEF Auto Parts Stores sold ABC tools. So, he called DEF's (retailer's) headquarters and asked to speak to the product manager who handled tools manufactured by ABC. Because he knew the title of the person he wanted to reach at the retailer's headquarters, they put him right through to that person.

George introduced himself to the retailer's product manager, described the benefits of his patented tool and asked if he would give him the contact information for the product manager for ABC Manufacturing so that he could discuss licensing his patent to them. Because he was professional in his approach and because he reached the right person, he was given the needed information. He then contacted the product manager at ABC (manufacturer) and told him he was referred by the product manager at DEF (retailer), which immediately got his attention. After sending a product brochure and a prototype, he received a proposed license agreement shortly thereafter. Using this method and the one mentioned in Step Two, George now had two proposed license agreements. Because of the competition between the two manufacturers for George's patent, he ended up with a very lucrative deal. His product is now sold all across the US, Canada, and in Europe. George worked smart and got the best possible license agreement. He is now working to license his latest invention. This can happen to you!

The company I contacted won't sign my

NDA and they require that I sign their submission documents before I can show my invention to them. What should I do?

Many companies will require you to complete and sign their submission documents before you can present your products to them. Even though the wording of these documents is a bit frightening to independent inventors, if you want to present your product to them there is no way around this formality. These documents have statements such as:

I am aware that your company may be working on a product similar to mine at this time.

I am aware that your company may have considered and declined a product similar to mine.

Different submission documents have other statements but these are typical. In most cases they will not sign your NDA and insist that what you present to them must be non-confidential. This is why it is of major importance to at least have a Provisional Patent Application filed before presenting to these manufacturers. Lots of manufacturers are very open to submissions from outside product developers but they almost always have these submission documents as a requirement before viewing new products and most of them require that your product be at least patent pending.

While these submission documents sound frightening to us who have spent time and money creating a new product, these documents are not designed to allow them to steal your product. Rather, they are designed to protect them against individuals who would sue them for stealing their products. It has been our experience that if indeed they have seen or worked on a similar product, they will freely discuss it with you during the meeting. And, this is always a possibility. In our years in this business we have discovered that most good ideas come to several people. If they discuss previous similar products with you it is an opportunity to show them how your product is better than what they considered earlier. As we said before, if you want to show your product to them and have a chance at licensing to them, you must sign their submission documents. No way around it.

That said, these signed documents go into their files and are probably never even looked at again unless you attempt legal action against them. There are some things you can do to protect yourself on your end in addition to your pending patent. After you have reached your contact by phone it is always a good idea to send an email confirming your appointment before you make the trip. And, after the meeting, no matter how the meeting has gone, always, always send a thank you note to the person who set up the meeting for you and to the people with whom you met. That note can be by email if you don't want to write an old-fashioned thank you note. These messages will document when and to whom you showed your invention if you should ever need this documentation. All of this correspondence, including the submission documents you signed, will become a part of your paper trail proving when you showed your invention to them.

One final caveat regarding signing submission documents: As we said earlier, there is no way that we know of to avoid signing them and we have not heard of anyone whose invention was ripped off due to signing one. But, bear in mind that if you are showing your inventions under protection of a Provisional Patent Application and have signed these submission documents, this is considered a public disclosure and will necessitate the filing of your Utility Patent Application within one year in order to avoid losing the right to file at all.

If you are able to obtain the license agreement and get the utility patent filed, either by the licensee or by filing it yourself, within that year, all should be well. If you are working with manufacturers toward a license agreement and your one-year period is coming to an end, you should go ahead and file the Utility Patent

Application in order to beat the one-year deadline. You can still have it written into your agreement that your licensee will take over the responsibility for obtaining the patent at the time of signing.

What should I take with me when I go to the appointment?

You should take your prototype and whatever is necessary to demonstrate it. Take a sell sheet, and, you should take a great written presentation. There is a free e-book on our website, www. AskTheInventors.com which shows step-by-step how to create a compelling written presentation for your invention.

Why do I need a written presentation if I am going in person to do an oral presentation?

Your written presentation serves several purposes. First, just the act of creating it will prepare you for your in-person presentation. It will make sure that you can answer the questions that the manufacturer will be likely to ask about your product; things such as the benefits (and here you will discuss benefits to the end user but also any benefits to him as the manufacturer), the cost to produce the item, what you believe it will retail for, and the market for this new product. So, just creating it will be excellent preparation for that important meeting.

Second, your written presentation will serve to remind them of all of the important points about your product after the meeting is over. It is very hard to grasp everything about something brand new on first seeing it. That written presentation will remind them of everything important that you have told them in the meeting.

Third, those who were at the meeting will be prepared to fully explain the new product to those who will be involved in the decision-making who were not at the meeting if they have your written presentation to share with them.

And last, if you are unable to meet with the manufacturer in person the written presentation will make the presentation for you and make your new product completely understandable to them. Sometimes, when we have worked on our product for a long time, we tend to forget that this is brand new to someone else and they may not "get" it from just looking at it the first time.

What should I expect at the meeting?

Okay, you have made the phone call and you have an appointment to show your product to a manufacturer for licensing. Now what? What happens at the meeting?

There can be anywhere from one to a dozen people sitting in on your meeting but it is usually two or three of the marketing and product development people in their company. When you schedule the meeting, tell them that you will be bringing presentation materials and ask how many people might attend. This will help you in planning how many written presentations to bring along. Always bring along enough written presentations for those at the meeting and two or three more in case there are others who might not be at the meeting who would be among the decision makers.

So, now the time is here and you have arrived for the meeting. Be sure to have enough of your business cards to give one to the receptionist when you enter the building and one for each person who attends the meeting, even though you will have business cards inside the presentation. You want them to be able to reach you!

You will be taken into the meeting room where some, if not all, of the attendees may already be waiting for you. Introduce yourself with a big smile and hand them your business card. They will probably give you their cards at that time, too. If others come into the room after you have begun, be sure to acknowledge them. Make frequent eye contact with each person in the room and always keep smiling. One of the main things you want to accomplish with this meeting, other than showing your product, is to create a friendly relationship with these individuals. Once you have established a warm environment it will be so much easier to get and keep their attention.

Be warm, be natural and behave as if you were speaking to personal friends. By this we don't mean back-slapping or physical contact of any kind other than the opening handshake. We mean the easy, conversational tone that you would use with a good friend. Maintain a professional tone but don't try to be anyone other than who you are.

Be sure to always be honest and admit if you don't know the answer to a question they ask. If you don't know the answer and try to wing it you may really make a fool of yourself. They will respect your honesty if you admit it when you don't know the answer. You can always say, "I'll do some research and try to find out."

When you present the product, do it with enthusiasm! Begin with a brief explanation of the story behind your invention, why you felt the need to develop it in the first place. If you have a compelling story of why you needed the product, it makes it easier for them to see why millions of others might also need and want it.

Explain why it is superior to other products that are being sold to serve the same purpose as your product. Maybe it is easier, faster, safer, less expensive, etc. Be sure to mention every possible benefit of your wonderful new product. If anyone says anything that you consider to be a negative, don't be defensive. Acknowledge their remark and indicate that you have respect for their opinions.

After you have made your oral presentation, which you will have basically memorized but you will be so familiar with it that you will deliver it as if it were extemporaneous, tell them what you want. You would not believe how many people get to that point and then leave it hanging. Tell them that you want to license your patent exclusively to them. This opens the door for that conversation.

They may ask what you expect in terms of a royalty percentage but, usually this doesn't come up in the first meeting. Be prepared in case it does. Sometimes it helps to have your own license agreement handy to give to them but if you do, be sure to tell them that this is just an opener and you are prepared to negotiate. When we do this we have our starter agreement filled in for 5% of wholesale. We always tell them that we are looking for a deal that is fair for all involved. We believe that if it isn't a good deal for everyone, it isn't good for anyone. This is not the time for digging your heels in. If you insist on a particular percentage at this juncture you could come across as a hard-nosed individual and someone that they will find difficult to work with.

I can't afford to have my prototype made and I can't make a prototype that looks like a shelf-ready product. What should I do?

What you should not do is panic. Manufacturers know that independent product developers do not have the ability or the resources to make a product that looks like it came right off the store shelf. A prototype has to do three things:

Show what the product is.

Show how the product works.

Show that the product does work.

If you can make a crude prototype from things that you already have at home or that you can get from someplace like Wal-Mart or Home Depot, the important thing is that it demonstrates what the product is and that it works.

It is sometimes possible to take something apart that you already have or that you can get cheaply from a garage sale or a discount store and get the parts you need in that way. For example, if you need a part that is used in an old clock or a toy, this is a good way to get parts you can use to fashion your prototype yourself.

If your prototype is something that you cannot make on your own, there are other alternatives. There are prototype designers who can make almost anything and, depending on the materials and labor involved, it may not be too expensive to have it made. If you do this, be sure to get them to sign a contractor's non-disclosure agreement before you proceed with them to make sure that there is no later discussion on the ownership of the product. These agreements should cover even if the designer suggests changes in the design so that there is no misunderstanding later that you are the sole owner of this intellectual property.

If you cannot find a convenient prototype designer in your area, it is often possible to get your prototype made by some other type of craftsman. For example, if your product is sewn, you could engage a seamstress; if it is made from wood or metal you could locate someone who works with those materials. Just remember to use that contractor's non-disclosure agreement, with whomever you engage to work for you.

My product will be made of plastic and I can't afford an injection mold. What can I do?

For prototypes that are to be made from plastic the eventual product will probably need an injection mold, something that costs thousands of dollars. But there are good alternatives for this kind of prototype, too. Investigate Rapid Prototyping. Randall Landreneau, of Complete Product Development in Clearwater, Florida explains the different types of rapid prototyping in this way, "Rapid prototyping refers to one of several processes used to turn a 3 dimensional CAD (computer assisted design) model of the part directly into the physical part. The most common processes used in rapid prototyping are Stereo Lithography (SLA), Fused Deposition Modeling (FDM), and Three Dimensional Printing (3DP).

In Stereo Lithography, a movable column positions itself in a special photosensitive resin so that a very thin layer of the liquid is on top of the column. Based on the CAD file of the part, a computer directs a laser to the exact areas of the liquid, which harden. The column then lowers a minute amount, providing another thin layer of liquid, which again gets hit by the laser. This goes on until the complete part is fully created.

In Fused Deposition Modeling, *a computer uses the CAD file to build the part using a very small extrusion of molten plastic, layer by layer.*

The latest addition is 3D Printing. *This process uses a special type of inkjet printer where a computer is directing the print heads to spray fine amounts of material, layer by layer, until the part is completely built.*

Any of these processes might only take a few hours to produce an actual part, but the part could cost several hundred dollars or more if it is relatively large. If you need a number of parts, and you need exact dimensions, you can have one part rapid prototyped, and then duplicate it as many times as you want with silicone molds using the information in my DVD How to Make Plastic Prototypes.

If your rapid prototype is for use with a silicone mold, the key is getting the best surface, which I have found easier with Stereo Lithography. The downside is that the STL part will be fairly brittle, so you have to be careful with it. With Fused Deposition Modeling and 3D printing, you can have the part made of a tough material, similar to ABS Plastic, but the surface is usually not as smooth.

3D Printing is the newest technology and is advancing quickly. The printers used are getting better and coming down in price. Some printers can build a part with different materials, like if the part has a more flexible surface where it is held."

As he mentioned in his description of rapid prototyping, Randall also has a wonderful DVD that teaches you how to make your own plastic prototypes. And, he has now expanded his offerings to other prototyping services. He does CAD design and rapid prototyping services as well as urethane casting. He can help you design your prototype if you don't have it completely worked out and he works with various materials. If you don't have someone who is convenient to you and who has the ability to do all of these things, you might wish to contact him. He works with inventors all across the US. His website is www.Complete Product Development.com.

Can I take my homemade prototype to the licensing meeting with a manufacturer?

Yes, you can. Just make it look as good as you possibly can but, as we said earlier, manufacturers do not expect your prototype to look like a shelf-ready product. That said; try to give it the look of your prospective licensee's other products. For example, when we were taking some improved portfolio designs to a large maker of school and office supplies, after we made the prototypes look as neat as we could (using their folders to make our prototypes), we went to their website, copied their logo that appeared on all of their products, and pasted it onto clear adhesive labels. Then we placed these labels on our prototypes to make them look as much as possible like their products.

They were clearly homemade prototypes but the fact that we used their materials and placed their logo on the prototypes helped them to visualize them as part of their line of products. And, they were impressed with our ingenuity.

In another example, we once took some folder innovations to another manufacturer of school and office products. In this case we also used their materials but we used folders that were made from vinyl. When we cut and pasted them together in a different configuration, they kept popping apart as the adhesive dried. In desperation we sewed the pieces together.

When we went to our presentation meeting we were a bit sheepish as we took out the prototypes and began explaining that we had been forced to sew them together because we hadn't been able to find an adhesive that would hold. We knew that if they decided to make the product they would use a heat sealing method that wasn't available to us. One member of the marketing team threw his hand up and with a big smile said, "Stop right there. Don't apologize for sewing those prototypes. That's exactly how we do things back in our prototyping room."

Whew! He made us feel a whole lot better about our homemade models! This is also an example of how friendly and how kind most of these people are once you have broken the ice with them.

Is it really important to make a prototype? Couldn't I just take my written presentation and maybe a virtual prototype on a DVD?

You could . . . but there are several big problems with that. Even though you probably feel positive that you know exactly how the product should be made and what it should be made of, you could get some surprises when you begin the prototyping process.

Here's an example of what we mean. When we were prototyping our first invention, Ghostline® poster board, we thought we knew exactly how it should be done. The final product was to be a poster board with a very faint grid that would be clearly visible up close for creating a poster project. But, we wanted the lines to virtually disappear from a short distance away. We imagined lines similar to very light pencil lines on the board. We tried several gray ink formulations but they all turned out too dark. Then, we began trying other colors. We tried light blue. Too dark. We tried white lines on a white board using a different shade of white for the lines. Too light. Then, we hit on yellow for the lines. We had our printer to make up some poster board with light yellow lines.

When we picked them up at his place of business, we were delighted. Under his fluorescent lighting the lines looked perfect! Then, we took the samples home and put them on the kitchen table, which is where most students would probably be making their posters. We couldn't believe our eyes! Where were the lines?? They simply disappeared under the incandescent lighting that most homes use. We wanted the lines to disappear, but not before we got the project onto the board!

We were back to the drawing board. We went

through eight or ten different combinations before we finally hit on the ink formulation that worked for us. If we had just assumed that the board would work with our first idea we would not have had anything patentable. And, manufacturers who are looking at licensing want something that is patented or at least patentable. They definitely want a developed invention, not just an idea.

That was a very simple invention and it required eight or ten tries to get it right. If you take an invention idea to a licensing meeting that you think will work but you haven't even tried it out, your chances of getting a license are very slim. While it is possible to file for a patent without creating a prototype, in our opinion it is foolhardy. If someone else finds flaws in your design and makes an improvement in the invention, it could be them making the money on it instead of you.

If your invention idea is so complicated or so expensive to prototype that you simply cannot take a prototype to the meeting, just be sure that you have researched the idea as thoroughly as you can and that you have the very best visual materials in your presentation. In this case your presentation should include anything that will showcase your invention that is not proprietary information in your patent application.

Will I get an advance payment when I sign the license agreement?

While it is sometimes possible to get advance payments when you sign a license agreement, many manufacturers are not willing to do this for a number of reasons. They are taking a large financial risk in taking on your new product. It will cost them a lot of money just to get it onto store shelves before they ever see any profit from it.

Remember that an advance is not a signing bonus. It is an advance against future royalties. Insisting on getting some of your royalties in advance may cause you to lose the deal if the manufacturer is not totally sold on and enthusiastic about the license agreement. We have received advances when we had more than one company that wanted the license because they wanted to sweeten the deal by giving us some of our royalties upfront. But, it all shakes out in the long run, so don't lose something that you have worked hard for by insisting on an advance.

The way to handle it is to include it in the preliminary license agreement that you bring to the meeting. But don't be surprised if you find it redlined out when you receive it back from their attorneys. What has usually happened with us in the past is that we gave them our preliminary license agreement and they may have used it as a guide to what we expected, but they prepared and presented us with their own license agreement.

Is there a sample license agreement so I can see what I need to present to them?

Yes. We have included a sample license

agreement that you can use to open up a licensing discussion with a manufacturer. We are not attorneys and this is only a suggested opening sample. As mentioned earlier, it is for the purpose of informing the manufacturer in general terms what you would like.

The following licensing agreement contains some of the basics of what should be included in a license agreement. You or your attorney may have other clauses that will pertain to your particular situation.

While the product will be essentially out of your hands as it relates to actually making and distributing it, you are able to exert some control in several key areas. These areas will be included in your license agreement.

SAMPLE LICENSING AGREEMENT

_____

_____

_____located at _____

_____

_____(hereinafter referred to as LICENSOR) has given _____

_____located at _____ (hereinafter referred to as LICENSEE) the exclusive production and marketing rights to his new product concept as herein described and as per drawings, patent applications, and/or prototype samples previous submitted. In exchange, LICENSEE agrees to pay LICENSOR a royalty in the amount and under the terms outlined in this Agreement.

PRODUCT DESCRIPTION:

ROYALTY PAYMENTS. A 5% (five percent) royalty, based on net selling price, will be paid by LICENSEE to LICENSOR on all sales of subject product line and all subsequent variations thereof by LICENSEE, its subsidiaries, and/or associate companies.

The term "net selling price" shall mean the price LICENSEE receives from its customers, less any discounts for volume, promotions, defects, or freight.

Royalty payments are to be made monthly by the 30th day of the month following shipment to LICENSEE's customers, and LICENSOR shall have the right to examine LICENSEE's books and records as they pertain thereto. Further, LICENSEE agrees to reimburse LICENSOR for any legal costs he may incur in collecting overdue royalty payments. LICENSEE agrees to pay LICENSOR a guaranteed minimum royalty of $_____annually and if the agreed upon amount is not recovered by LICENSEE through sales during the annual term, such overage in royalty payments as may occur is not recoverable from future royalty years.

2. TERRITORY. LICENSEE shall have the right to market this product(s) throughout the United States, its possessions, and territories, Canada and Mexico. It may do so through any legal distribution channels it desires and in any manner it sees fit without prior approval from LICENSOR. However, LICENSEE agrees that it will not knowingly sell to parties who

intend to resell the product(s) outside of the licensed territory.

ADVANCE PAYMENT. Upon execution of this Agreement, LICENSEE will make a nonrefundable payment to LICENSOR of $_____ which shall be construed as an advance against future earned royalties.

COPYRIGHT, PATENT, AND TRADEMARK NOTICES. LICENSEE agrees that on the product, its packaging and collateral material there will be printed notices of any patents issued or pending and applicable trademark and/or copyright notices showing the LICENSOR as the owner of said patents, trademarks or copyrights under exclusive license to LICENSEE.

At its expense LICENSEE agrees to defend all infringement lawsuits that may be brought against it or its subsidiaries, and diligently enforce the LICENSED PATENTS and the LICENSED TRADEMARKS against all infringements brought to its attention.

In the event there has been no previous

registration or patent application for the licensed product(s), LICENSEE may, at LICENSEE's discretion and expense, make such application or registration in the name of the INVENTOR. However, LICENSEE agrees that at termination or expiration of this Agreement, LICENSEE will be deemed to have assigned, transferred and conveyed to LICENSOR all trade rights, equities, goodwill, titles or other rights in and to licensed product which may have been attained by the LICENSEE. Any such transfer shall be without consideration than as specified in this Agreement.

TERMS AND WARRANTS. This Agreement shall be considered to be in force for so long as LICENSEE continues to sell the original product line or subsequent extensions and/or variations thereof. Further, LICENSOR agrees that, for the life of this Agreement, he will not create and/or provide directly competitive products to another manufacturer or distributor without giving the right of first refusal to LICENSEE.

PRODUCT DESIGNS. LICENSOR agrees to furnish conceptual product designs, if requested, for the initial product line and all subsequent variations and extensions at no charge to LICENSEE. In addition, if requested, LICENSOR will assist in the design of packaging, point-of-purchase materials, displays, etc. at no charge to LICENSEE.

However, costs for finished art, photography, typography, mechanical preparation, etc. will be borne by LICENSEE.

QUALITY OF MERCHANDISE. LICENSEE agrees that Licensed product(s) will be produced and distributed in accordance with federal, state and local laws. LICENSEE further agrees to submit a sample of said product(s), its cartons, containers, and packing material to LICENSOR for approval (which approval shall not be reasonably withheld). Any item not specifically disapproved at the end of fifteen (15) working days after submission shall be deemed to be approved. The product(s) may not thereafter be materially changed without approval of the LICENSOR.

DEFAULT, BANKRUPTCY, VIOLATION, ETC.

In the event LICENSEE does not commence to manufacture, distribute and sell product(s) within six months after the execution of this Agreement, LICENSOR, in addition to all other remedies available to him, shall have the option of canceling this Agreement. Should this event occur, to be activated by registered letter, LICENSEE agrees not to continue with the product's development and is obligated to return all prototype samples and drawings to LICENSOR.

In the event LICENSEE files a petition in bankruptcy, or if the LICENSEE becomes insolvent, or makes an assignment for the benefit of creditors, the license granted hereunder shall terminate automatically without the requirement of a written notice. No further sales of licensed product(s) may be made by LICENSEE, its receivers, agents, administrators or assigns without the express written approval of the LICENSOR.

If LICENSEE shall violate any other obligations under the terms of this Agreement, and upon receiving written notice of such violations by LICENSOR, LICENSEE shall have thirty (30) days to remedy such violation. If this has not been done, LICENSOR shall have the option of canceling the Agreement upon ten (10) days written notice. If this event occurs, all sales activity must cease and any royalties owing are immediately due.

LICENSEE'S RIGHT TO TERMINATE. Notwithstanding anything contained in this Agreement, LICENSEE SHALL HAVE THE ABSOLUTE RIGHT TO CANCEL THIS Agreement at any time by providing sixty (60) days written notice to LICENSOR of his decision to discontinue the sale of the product(s) covered by this Agreement. This cancellation shall be without recourse from LICENSOR other than for the collection of any royalty payment that may be due him. This notice of cancellation does not relieve LICENSEE of responsibility for payment of any minimum royalty due for that license year.

INDEMNIFICATION. LICENSEE agrees to obtain, at its own expense, product liability insurance for at least $2,000,000 combined single unit for LICENSEE and LICENSOR against claims, suits, loss or damage arising out of any alleged defect in the licensed product(s). As proof of such insurance, LICENSEE will submit to LICENSOR a fully paid certificate of insurance naming LICENSOR as an insured party. This submission is to be made before any licensed product is distributed or sold.

NO PARTNERSHIP, ETC. This Agreement shall be binding upon the successors and assigns of the parties hereto. Nothing contained in this Agreement shall be construed to place the parties in the relationship of legal representatives, partners, or joint venturers. Neither LICENSOR nor LICENSEE shall have the power to bind or obligate in any manner whatsoever, other than as per this Agreement.

GOVERNING LAW. This Agreement shall be construed in accordance with the laws of the state of _____.

IN WITNESS WHEREOF, the parties hereto have signed this Agreement as of the day and year written below.

_____

_____LICENSEE

DATE: _____

_____

LICENSOR

DATE: _____

____

***

Having your contract worded in such a way that you are to be paid based on the net profit, rather than the net selling price can eliminate your royalty. There are ways that a company's books can be done so as to never show a profit and therefore never have to pay you. Be sure your royalty is paid on the net selling price, not net profit.

As we previously mentioned, the above sample licensing agreement is extremely basic and not to be considered to contain some important clauses that you will need in your agreement. These are the things that a contract attorney would handle for you. For example, no mention is made of the term of the agreement as it relates to you. You should be able to renew the agreement at specific intervals, every two to four years, in order to renegotiate terms or to discontinue the agreement if you wish. Also, your right to audit the records of your licensee should be clearly defined regarding what can be audited and at what intervals. These and other important details are good reasons for having the best contract attorney you can get for writing and negotiating the terms of your agreement.

STEP FOUR:
OVERCOMING OBSTACLES

WHAT IF I CAN'T GET A FACE-TO-FACE MEETING?

Should I send my prototype and presentation if I cannot meet them in person?

You should, but not until you have called and spoken to whomever you are sending the information. If you skip the call is it a BIG MISTAKE! If you send unsolicited material to a manufacturer without having spoken to them and signed and submitted their submission documents they probably will not even look at it. If you are very lucky they may send it back to you unopened. If you are not so lucky they will simply toss it into the trash. You do not want that to happen!

How can I prevent that?

You can prevent it by doing your homework. Find out to whom you should speak and call them before you send anything. It is a rookie mistake to simply send your materials unsolicited. They will recognize that you are not behaving in a professional manner and it is a good bet that they will dismiss anything you have sent.

In Step Three there are examples of how to make the phone call to get the appointment. If you were not able to go to the tradeshow but did join the potential licensee's trade association this is an important thing to mention in the phone call when you must send your prototype and written presentation instead of taking them in person. It may make the difference between getting through to the correct person and failure. If you tell the receptionist that you belong to their trade association and would like to speak to Mr. New Product Developer she will probably put you through when she might not if you do not have that credential to back you up.

Can I send it regular mail?

You can, but that would be a mistake. You want your package and presentation to get the attention it deserves. Regular mail is for ordinary non-important things. You want your package to stand out and get noticed. The way to make that happen is to send it in an attention-getting way. Send it FedEX or Overnight USPS! When a FedEX or Overnight USPS package or envelope arrives it garners attention. The recipient automatically thinks, "This must be something really important to have been sent FedEX or Overnight USPS!" You can be sure it will be opened first!

To whom should I send it?

This is another place where you will benefit by having done your research. If it is a smaller company then you should send it to the President of the company, whose name you know. You may be surprised that when you call a small company the receptionist is likely to put you right through to the president when you ask for him by name. Let's assume that when you spoke to him you piqued his interest in your product. After he receives your package he will look it and your presentation over. If he agrees with you that this might be a great addition to his product line he will either contact you himself or he will have one of his employees contact you. You can be sure that if the president of the company hands off the responsibility of contacting you to an employee it will get done.

If you are approaching a midsized to large company then you should find out what they call the department responsible for bringing in new products. It might be the New Products Division, R & D (Research and Development) or even simply the Marketing Department. Regardless of what they call it find out the name of the person who heads that department and send it to him.

When a company has a New Products

Department it is important to go through them and not around them. Going around them is a sure way to get shut down before you even have a chance to show them what a great product you have and what a perfect fit it is with their existing product line.

Many midsized to large companies have something we call Not Invented Here Disease (NIHD). The new products division or the R & D department are very protective of their jobs. They hate to be shown up by outside product developers. It is their job to come up with great new products for their company and if you are not careful they will dismiss your idea regardless of how good it might be because they did not come up with it.

In order to avoid being contaminated by NIHD it is important to be very diplomatic in how they are approached. If you schmooze and make friends with the person in charge of the New Products Division it is possible that they will take on your product as their "find" for the company and usher it through the proper channels. Always be cognizant of their feelings and their egos. Never say anything that could be construed as critical of why they didn't think of this.

Can I just hire a licensing agent to do all of this for me?

That sounds like the easiest way to do this, right? Wrong! Legitimate licensing agents are few and far between. Some sectors of the market have no licensing agents at all. Lots of companies advertise that they will do it all for you. All you have to do is sit back and collect tons of money. We wish it worked that way but it does not. The companies that advertise that they will do everything for you are unethical. They begin by offering a free inventor's kit, then, they ask for a fairly small amount of money to proceed. Then they come back for a larger amount of money and it just goes on and on as they keep asking for more and more money. In the meantime, your invention is going nowhere.

You know that old saying that if something sounds too good to be true it probably is? That is absolutely true in this case. Most, if not all, of the companies that advertise that they will do it all for you (for a fee) are scammers. They are only out to get your money. The USPTO tells us that the scam invention promotion business is a multi-billion dollar business in the US alone.

Are there any legitimate licensing agents?

Yes, there are. If your product is a toy or game there are a few legitimate agents as well as number of scammers in that sector of the market. On the Resources page of our website, www.asktheinventors.com, we list two legitimate toy and game agents. The toy and game sector of the market is the only one we know of that works almost exclusively through agents.

If your product is not a toy or a game and you hope to find a legitimate agent the best way is to contact your potential licensee and ask them if they work with agents. If they do they will be happy to provide you with the agent's contact information. At that point you contact the agent and pitch your product to them. Be aware that if you use an agent they will share a portion of your royalties if they are able to get a licensing agreement for you.

I really need someone else to do this for me. Is there a way to find out if there is an agent in the category of my invention?

If you really feel that you need someone else to represent your product for licensing, phone the companies that you have targeted as potential licensees and ask them if they work with agents. If they do, they will give you the contact information for the agents with whom they work. Then, contact them and submit your invention to them.

For example, we do know of a legitimate company that licenses household inventions. It is Monashee Marketing and the gentleman to contact is Warren Tuttle. He can be reached at http://www.monasheemarketing.com/submission.html.

There are probably others like Mr. Tuttle in other product categories but they have not come to our attention at this writing.

I've tried and I just can't find anyone legitimate to represent my product for me. What should I do?

That's okay! You are your own best agent anyway. If you represent yourself you do not have to share your royalties with anyone else.

No one understands your product the way you do. You know why you invented it, why it is needed, and why if you need it millions of others undoubtedly need it too. Your invention is your baby! No one loves it the way you do. No one can be as passionate and enthusiastic about it as you can. Enthusiasm is contagious! Go and infect potential licensees with your enthusiasm for your product.

What if I am too shy to go to a big company?

You are not. Believe us when we say that. Mary (co-author of this book) was one of the most painfully shy people you could ever meet. When we were first selling Ghostline® out of the trunk of her car to local office supplies and teacher stores she wouldn't even get out of the car.

That all changed in a second when we were invited to have a table at a small tradeshow specifically for school and office products. When the people started walking into the show she turned into a carnival barker. She was so proud of "our baby" that her enthusiasm couldn't be contained. When she had the opportunity to explain the benefits of our product her passion for our product exploded! Shyness disappeared. She was talking one-on-one telling people about Ghostline®. That is the way it will be for you too.

Whether you are meeting with only one person or several, it is just you explaining to people, who are already interested in your product or you wouldn't be there, why your product is great and will make money for them. You can and should do this yourself!

STEP FIVE: SEALING THE DEAL

CAN I NEGOTIATE MY LICENSE AGREEMENT MYSELF?

Do I need to get an attorney involved? If so, at what point?

You have come a long way. You have met with representatives of a manufacturing company and they want to sign a license agreement with you. Woohoo! This is what you have been working toward for a long time now. This is the time to work smart to get the best possible agreement that you can get for yourself.

Up to now you have probably handled pretty much everything yourself but now it's getting a bit dicey because you are about to be asked to sign a legally binding contract. In most cases, the potential licensee will make the first move by presenting you with a license agreement written by their attorneys.

Even though you are watching your budget and may dislike having to pay another attorney at this point, we strongly urge you, not only to hire an attorney for this, but to hire a contract attorney. Just as your patent attorney specializes in the writing and prosecution of patents and trademarks, a contract attorney is uniquely qualified to write good, strong contracts. There are a few patent attorneys who are also contract attorneys. This is the best of both worlds because these attorneys are well versed in what should and should not be included in a licensing agreement for intellectual property.

When you read over it, if you are not an attorney, it may look just fine to you. When we received our first license agreement we couldn't see a thing wrong with it but we sent it to an attorney to look at it for us just because it seemed the right thing to do. After all, the manufacturer had a team of attorneys who wrote the agreement so we needed to at least have someone to look at it to tell us if it was okay for us to sign it. We couldn't believe our eyes when he sent it back to us! It was redlined all over! There were so many things he took exception to that we were really shocked because we hadn't seen any of it when we read over it.

When a manufacturer has the agreement written by his attorneys they naturally are looking out for his best interests and that's as it should be. But, you need no less for yourself at this very important time. If we had signed the agreement as it was originally written we would have had some difficult things to live with for the life of the agreement unless we could get them to agree to the changes. The attorney we sent the agreement to was not a contract attorney and he did a pretty good job of looking out for our interests. We ended up with a much fairer contract than we would have if we had signed the original agreement. But, he overlooked a couple of things that a contract attorney would not have overlooked. Thus, we have had to deal with a few problems that would not have occurred if we had gotten our contract overseen by a contract attorney who was familiar with license agreements.

All of this is to tell you that, while we are all about saving money all the way down the line during the inventing process, when it is time to sign a license agreement, it is time to get the best contract attorney you can find. You have done your own negotiating up to now. Whatever it costs to get his help at this point will be negligible over the life of your agreement and it may save you many thousands of dollars and much frustration. Getting the best representation you can in obtaining a good license agreement won't cost you . . . it will pay you in the long run.

How can I find a contract attorney?

If you have a local inventor's club or association, that's an excellent place to start.

Someone in your organization may know a good contract attorney. Your patent attorney or patent agent may recommend a contract attorney. You can also contact your state bar association to get referrals. And, as a last resort, you can Google "Contract Attorney". There are numerous links but if you use this method be sure to check the credentials and history of anyone you find in this way unless you get the referral through a website that you already know and trust. It's an added bonus if you can find a patent attorney who is also a contract attorney because these individuals are well-versed both in contracts and patents.

SUMMARY

WHY DID WE CHOOSE LICENSING?

Did we have the financial resources to start a new business?

No, we did not. We were both working full-time and handling all of our responsibilities to our husbands and children. Our small amount of savings went into getting started, making our prototypes and getting the first batches of Ghostline® made so that we could peddle it to local office supply and teacher stores from the trunk of our car. We definitely did not have the thousands of dollars it would have taken to start a business.

Could we overcome the One Product Vendor Roadblock ourselves?

No, we could not. And believe us, we tried! We contacted all the big retail stores over and over trying to get appointments to show them our wonderful new product. The answer was always the same: If Ghostline® is your only product you will need to place it with a distributor with whom we already purchase many products before we will even look at it.

The One Vendor Roadblock we encountered may as well have been the Great Wall of China! We were not getting around it!

Were we willing to be tied down by a business and all the details of running a business?

As we mentioned before we both had full-time jobs at the time we developed Ghostline®. We did not want to take on yet another full-time job which is what it would have been.

We both were business owners already and had the knowledge and skill to run a business we just didn't want to. We were what are called late bloomers when we came up with Ghostline®. We wanted to slow down, not start anew!

And, we subscribed to the philosophy that has been attributed to John D. Rockefeller in which he said, "I'd rather earn 1% off 100 people's efforts than 100% of my own."

Did we have the ability to give our product immediate wide distribution?

No, we were lucky to be selling small batches of Ghostline® to local office supply and teacher supply stores. We couldn't get the time of day from the big box stores like Wal-Mart, K-Mart, CVS, Walgreens, Kroger, etc. We absolutely could not get nationwide distribution.

Did we have the financial resources to enforce our patents?

Not even close! Patent enforcement lawsuits can cost millions! Even worse, we knew we had a company ripping us off at the time we were offering Ghostline® for licensing. We knew the rip-off company would have to be stopped and we knew we couldn't afford to do that. The rip-off company was also aware that we were just two sisters who did not have the financial resources to make them stop. Our only hope was to find a licensee who was willing to make them stop.

Was our licensee able to overcome all these obstacles for us?

Yes! Our licensee simply added Ghostline® to their existing product line. They already had wide distribution and Ghostline® allowed them to expand their distribution even more since they were the only source for it.

Our licensee loved Ghostline® and the opportunities it offered them so much that they were willing to take on the responsibility for enforcing the patent even though they were aware there was a rip-off company that had to be stopped. They agreed to sue the rip-off company the day the patent issued and they did.

It all turned out well. The rip-off company loved Ghostline® too and the expanded market it provided and they agreed to take a sublicense rather than stop making it. The result is we receive the same royalty from the sublicense as we do from our primary licensee. All good!

Last words:

In the same way that there are a lot of routes on a roadmap to get you to the same destination, there are lots of ways to accomplish licensing of your product. We have shared with you the method that has worked for us repeatedly. The things we have learned are that licensing requires a very good product for which there will be a large market, good protection of that product so that the licensee will have an advantage over his competitors in the marketplace, and the finesse to locate and entice the prospective licensees to desire a license agreement. There is certainly some luck involved regarding timing, etc., but skill far outweighs luck when it comes to licensing new products. Hundreds of thousands of good products and good patents languish because that final step of obtaining the license agreement didn't happen. We hope this book will enable you to step out and make it happen for your great new product!

ABOUT THE AUTHORS

SISTERS **BARBARA RUSSELL PITTS** AND **MARY** Russell Sarao are co-authors of *The Everything Inventions and Patents Book*, which was published in December 2005 by Adams Media and Inventing on a Shoestring Budget, which was first published in 2006 with a new updated and revised edition released in 2012. Barbara has written for the *United Inventors' Association Newsletter* and the *Ask the Inventors* website, www.asktheinventors.com, an information service they offer at no charge for inventors. Mary has written two popular e-books, "*Super Easy Guide to Step-by-Step Patent Searching Online*" and "*Create a Compelling Presentation for your Invention*," that are offered without cost to visitors to their website, www.asktheinventors. com. She has also written for that website and for the Texas Inventors' Association Website, www.txinventors.com.

Successful inventors and recognized experts on the subject, Barbara and Mary have lectured extensively on the different areas of inventing and marketing at seminars, workshops and organizations around the country as well as appearing on radio and television talk shows. In 2001, they were featured inventors in the documentary film, "The Big Idea."

Barbara has served on the board of directors and as secretary of the executive committee of the United Inventors Association and is a past president and current board member of the Texas Inventors' Association. Mary has served on the Board of Directors of the United Inventors Association and is a past president and current board member of the Texas Inventors' Association. In July 2003 and again in January 2006 Barbara and Mary were the subject of articles in the *Dallas Morning News* about their passion for assisting novice inventors. The first article was picked up by the wire services and carried in newspapers nationwide. The sisters have been written about in books by other authors on inventing. Some of these are *The 12 Amazing Secrets of Millionaire Inventors*, by Harvey Reese, *The Right Sisters*, by Julia Rhodes, and *Hardcore Inventing*, by Ellie Crowe.

Their first invention, Ghostline®, has sold retail in excess of $200 million dollars since it was licensed in 1996.

Both are native Oklahomans who now live in the Dallas, Texas area.

PATENT & TRADEMARK
DEPOSITORY LIBRARIES

Alabama

Auburn University Libraries (205) 844-1737
Birmingham Public Library (205) 226-3620

Alaska

Anchorage: Z.J. Loussac Public Library
(907) 562-7323

Arizona

Tempe: Noble Library, Arizona State University
(602) 965-7010

Arkansas

Little Rock: Arkansas State Library (501) 682-2053

California

Los Angeles Public Library (213) 228-7220
Sacramento: California State Library (916) 654-0069

San Diego Public Library (619) 236-5813
San Francisco Public Library (415) 557-4488
Sunnyvale Patent Clearinghouse (408) 730-7290

Colorado

Denver Public Library (303) 640-8847

Connecticut

New Haven: Free Public Library (203) 946-7452
Hartford: Hartford Public Library (860) 543-8628

Delaware

Newark: University of Delaware Library (302) 831-2965

District of Columbia

Howard University Libraries (202) 806-7252

Florida

Fort Lauderdale: Broward County Main Library (305) 357-7444
Miami-Dade Public Library (305) 375-2665
Orlando: University of Central Florida Libraries (407) 823-2562
Tampa Campus Library, University of South

florida (813) 974-2726

Georgia

Atlanta: Price Gilbert Memorial Library, Georgia Institute of Technology (404) 894-4508

Hawaii

Honolulu: Hawaii State Public Library System (808) 586-3477

Idaho

Moscow: University of Idaho Library (208) 885-6235

Illinois

Chicago Public Library (312) 747-4450

Indiana

Indianapolis-Marion County Public Library (317) 269-1741
West Lafayette: Siegesmund Engineering Library, Purdue University (317) 494-2872

Iowa

Des Moines: State Library of Iowa (515) 281-4118

Kansas

Wichita: Ablah Library, Wichita State Library
(316) 689-3155

Kentucky

Louisville Free Public Library (502) 574-1611

Louisiana

Baton Rouge: Troy H. Middleton Library,
Louisiana State University
(504) 388-8875

Maine

Orono: Raymond H. Fogler Library, University
of Maine (207) 581-1691

Maryland

College Park: Engineering and Physical
Sciences Library, University of Maryland
(301) 405-9157

Massachusetts

Amherst: Physical Sciences Library, University
of Massachusetts (413) 545-1370
Boston Public Library (617) 536-5400, ext. 265

Michigan

Ann Arbor: Media Union, University of Michigan (734) 647-5735
Big Rapids: Abigail S. Timme Library, Ferris State University (616) 592-3602
Detroit Public Library (313) 833-3379

Minnesota

Minneapolis Public Library and Information Center (612) 630-6120

Mississippi

Jackson: Mississippi Library Commission (601) 961-4111

Missouri

Kansas City: Linda Hall Library (816) 363-4600
St. Louis Public Library (314) 241-2288, ext. 390

Montana

Butte: Montana college of Mineral Science and Technology Library (406) 496-4281

Nebraska

Lincoln: Engineering Library, University of Nebraska-Lincoln (402) 472-3411

Nevada

Las Vegas: Clark County Library (Not
Yet Operational)
Reno: University of Nevada-Reno Library
(702) 784-6500

New Hampshire

Concord: New Hampshire State Library
(603) 271-2239

New Jersey

Newark Public Library (973) 733-7779
Piscataway: Library of Science and Medicine,
Rutgers University (908) 445-2895

New Mexico

Albuquerque: University of New Mexico
General Library (505) 277-4412

New York

Albany: New York State Library (518) 474-5355
Buffalo and Erie County Public Library
(716) 858-7101
New York Public Library (the Research
Libraries) (212) 592-7000
Rochester: Center Library of Rochester and
Monroe County (716) 428-8110

Stony Brook: Melville Library, Room 1101, SUNY at Stony Brook (516) 632-7148

West Virginia

Morgantown: Evansdale Library, West Virginia University (304) 293-4695, Ext. 5113

Wisconsin

Madison: Kurt F. Wendt Library, University of Wisconsin-Madison (608) 262-6845
Milwaukee Public Library (414) 286-3051

Wyoming

Cheyenne: Wyoming State Library
(307) 777-7281

INVENTOR CLUBS

IF YOUR CLUB IS NOT LISTED HERE PLEASE notify us so that we may include it. If your club contact information has changed please let us know. The following list is in alphabetical order by state. Canadian clubs are shown at the end of the list.

Alabama

Alabama Inventors Club
Anderson, Al 35610
Tel: 256 229 5551
Tel: 256 331 5270
E-mail: Francisco@snowmasters.com

Invent Alabama
Alabaster, Al 35077
Tel: 866 745 6319

Arizona

Arizona Inventors Association

Glendale, AZ 85312
Tel: 800 229 6787
E-mail: exdir@azinventors.org
Web: www.azinventors.org

Arkansas

Arkansas Inventors' Network
Little Rock, AR 72215
Tel 501 247 6125
E-mail: chad@collinsconsultinginc.com
Web: www.arkansasinvents.org

Inventors Congress, Inc.
Tel: 501 229 4515

California

Inventors Forum
Huntington Beach, CA 99264
Tel: 714 540 2491
Tel: 562 464 0069
Web: www.inventorsforum.org

Inventors Alliance – Mountain View
Mountain View, CA 94039
Tel 650 964 1576
E-mail: President7@inventorsalliance.org
Web: www.inventorsalliance.org

InventNET Forum
Stanton, CA 90680
E-mail: info@inventnet.com
Contra Costa Inventors club
Pleasant Hill, CA 94523
Tel: 510 934 1331

San Diego Inventors Forum
San Marcos, CA 92069
Tel: 760 591 9608
E-mail: asquared@cts.com
Web: www.sdinventors.org

Bruce Sawyer Center
Santa Rosa, CA 95405
Tel: 707 524 1773
E-mail: sbdc1@ap.net

Invention Accelerator Workshop
San Diego, CA 92127
Tel: 858 451 1028
E-mail: sdinventor@gmail.com

Inventors Alliance – Northern California
Redding, CA 96001
Tel: 530 241 5222
Tel: 530 241 8427
E-mail: sagn@charter.net

Web: www.inventorsnorcal.org

Idea to Market Network
Santa Rosa, CA 95406
Tel: 800 ITM 3210
E-mail: sidnee@ap.net
Web: www.ideatomarket.org

Colorado

Rocky Mountain Inventors' Association
Denver, CO 80222
Tel: 303 831 4133
E-mail: Joshua@amanagementgroup.com
Web: www.rminventor.org

Connecticut

Christian Inventors Association
Shelton, CT 06484
Tel: 203 924 9538
E-mail: pal@ourpal.com
Web: www.ourpal.com

Danbury Innovators
Danbury, CT
Tel: 203 426 4205
E-mail: Iambest2@juno.com

Innovators Guild

Danbury, CT 06811
Tel: 203 790 8235
E-mail: rfaulkner@snet.net

Inventors Association of Connecticut
Rowayton, CT 06853
Tel: 203 866 0720
E-mail: iact@inventus.org
Web: www.inventus.org

Delaware

Early Stage East
Wilmington, DE 19806
Tel: 302 777 2460
E-mail: info@earlystageeast.org

Delaware Entrepreneurs Forum
Tel: 302 652 4241

District of Columbia

Inventors Network of the Capital Area
Annandale, VA 22003
Tel: 703 203 2710
E-mail: info@dcinventors.org
Web: www.dcinventors.org

Florida

Inventors Society of South Florida

Delray Beach, FL 33482
Tel: 973 219 9627
E-mail: info@inventorssociety.net
Web: www.inventorssociety.net

Edison Inventors Association, Inc.
Ft. Myers, FL 33919
Tel: 239 267 9746
E-mail: drghn@aol.com
Web: www.edisoninventors.org

Emerald Coast Inventors' Society
Pensacola, FL 32514
Tel: 904 455 4641

Inventors Council of Central Florida
Orlando, FL 32806
Tel: 407 859 4855
E-mail: drdavidflinchbaugh@bellsouth.net

Palm Isles Inventors Group
Boynton Beach, FL 33437
Tel: 561 739 9259
Tel: 561 739 9439

Space Coast Inventors Guild
Indian Harbor Beach, FL 32937
Tel: 321 773 4031

Tel: 321 506 3896
E-mail: del@nc-9.com
Tampa Bay Inventors Council
Largo, FL 33770
Tel: 727 548 5083
E-mail: goodharbinger@yahoo.com
Web: www.tbic.us

Georgia

Inventor Association of Georgia, Inc.
Marietta, GA 30062
Tel: 404 323 8686
Web: www.geogiainventors.com/index.php

Hawaii

Hawaii-International Inventors
Association, Inc.
Honolulu, HI 96816
Tel: 808 523 5555
E-mail: sakodaesq@aol.com

Idaho

East Idaho Inventors Forum
Tel: 208 346 6763
E-mail: wordinjj@ida.net

Illinois

Chicago 1st Black Inventors Entrepreneurs

Chicago, IL 60608
Tel: 312 850 4710
E-mail: cfbieo@sbcglobal.net
Web: www.cfbieo.org

Inventors' Council
Tel: 312 939 3329
E-mail: patent@donmoyer.com
Web: www.donmoyer.com

Illinois Innovators & Inventors' Club
Edwardsville, IL 62025
Tel: 618 656 7445
E-mail: inventorclub@yahoo.com
Web: ilinventor.tripod.com

Indiana

Indiana Inventors Association
Fishers, IN 46037
Tel: 317 842 8438
E-mail: dzedonis@comcast.net

Iowa

Iowa Inventors Group
Cedar Rapids, IA 52410
Tel: 206 350 6035
E-mail: info@iowainventorsgroup.org
Web: www.iowainventorsgroup.org

Drake University Inventure Program
Des Moines, IA 50311
Tel: 515 271 2655

Kansas

Inventors Association of South Central Kansas
Wichita, KS 67205
Tel: 316 721 1866
E-mail: inventor@inventkansas.com
Web: www.inventkansas.com

Kansas Association of Inventors
Hoisington, KS 67544
Tel: 316 653 2165
E-mail: clayton@hoisington.com

Mid-America Inventors Association
Kansas City, KS 66110
Tel: 913 495 9465
E-mail: midamerica-inventors@kc.rr.com
Web: www.midamerica-inventors.com

Inventors club of Kansas City
Overland Park, KS 66224
Tel: 913 268 0983
E-mail: steve@theickc.org
Web: www.inventorclubsofkc.org

Kentucky

Inventors Association of Middle Tennessee and
Southern Kentucky
Tel: 615 681 6462
E-mail: inventorsassocation@hotmail.com
Web: www.iamt.us

Central Kentucky Inventors Council, Inc.
Lexington, KY 40517
E-mail: donskaggs@ckic.org
Web: www.ckic.org

Louisiana

Louisiana Inventors Association
Baton Rouge, LA 70816
Tel: 225 752 3783
E-mail: info@recyclecycle.com

International Society of Product Design
Engineers/Entrepreneurs
Oberlin, LA 70655
Tel: 337 639 2409
E-mail: rwhitf1754@aol.com

Maine

Portland Inventors Forum
Department Industrial Co-op

Orono, ME 04469
Tel: 207 581 2201
E-mail: jsward@maine.edu
Web: www.umaine.edu/dic

Massachusetts

Cape Cod Inventors Association
Wellfleet, MA 02667
Tel: 508 349 1628
E-mail: cdwbauer@.msn.com
Greater Boston Inventors Association
Pepperal, MA 01463
Tel: 978 433 2397
E-mail: crholt@aol.com
Web: www.inventne.org

Innovators Resource Network
Shutesbury, MA 01072
Tel: 413 259 2006
E-mail: info@irnetwork.org
Web: www.irnetwork.org

Worchester Area Inventors
Upton, MA 01568
Tel: 508 529 3552
Tel: 508 791 0226
E-mail: swcei@aol.com

Inventors Association of New England
Lexington, MA 02420
Tel: 781 274 8500
E-mail: rhausslein@rcn.com
Web: www.inventne.org

National Collegiate Inventors and
Innovators Alliance
Hadley, MA 01035
Tel: 413 587 2172
E-mail: info@nciia.org
Web: www.nciia.org

Michigan

Inventors' Council of Mid-Michigan
Lennon, MI 48449
Tel: 810 659 6416
E-mail: msovis@comcast.net
Web: www.inventorscouncil.org

InventorEd, Inc.
Grand Blanc, MI 48439
Tel: 810 936 4356
E-mail: rjriley@InventorEd.org
Web: www.rjriley.com/icmm

The Entrepreneur Network
Ann Arbor, MI 48113

Tel: 734 663 8000
E-mail: edzimmer@TENonline.org
Web: www.tenonline.org

Muskeogon Inventors Network
Muskegon, MI 49441
Tel: 866 719 1290
E-mail: orvilles@comcast.net
Web: www.muskegoninventorsnetwork.org

Grand Rapids Inventors Network
Grand Rapids, MI 49507
E-mail: GRINventors@gmail.com
Web: www.grinventors.org

Mid Michigan Inventors Group
Midland, MI 48642
Tel: 989 832 1995
E-mail: contact@midmig.org
Web: www.midmig.org

Minnesota

Society of Minnesota Inventors
Coon Rapids, MN
Tel: 763 753 2766
E-mail: pgpent@yahoo.com

Inventors' Network

Excelsior, MN 55331
Tel: 651 602 3175
Web: www.inventorsnetwork.org

Minnesota Inventors Congress
Redwood Falls, MN 56283
Tel: 800 468 3681
E-mail: deb@minnesotainventorscongress.org
Web: www.minnesotainventorscongress.org

Mississippi

Mississippi SBDC Inventor Assistance
Tel: 662 915 5001
Tel: 601 232 5001
E-mail: blantrip@olemiss.edu
Web: www.olemiss.edu/depts/mssbdc/invent.
html

Missouri

Center for Business & Economic Development
Springfield, MO 65804
Tel: 417 836 5671
E-mail: geraldudell@smsu.edu
Web: www.inventorsalliance.org

Mid-America Inventors Association
Kansas city, KS 66110
Tel: 913 495 9465

E-mail: midamerica-inventors@kc.rr.com
Web: www.midamerica-inventors.com

Inventors Association of St. Louis
St. Louis, MO 63141
Tel: 314 432 1291
E-mail: dayjobIASL@webtv.net
Web: www.communityconnection.org

Women Inventors Project
Hazelwood, MO 63042
Tel: 314 432 1291
Inventors Alliance – Mountain View
Tel: 913 825 2587
Web: www.inventorsclubofkc.org

Montana

Blue Sky Inventors
Billings, MT 59102
Tel: 406 259 9110

Montana Inventors Association
Bozeman, MT 59715
Tel: 406 586 1541
Yellowstone Inventors
Tel: 406 259 9110

Nebraska

Lincoln Inventors Association
Brainard, NE 68626
Tel: 402 545 2179
Web: http://assist.ded.state.ne.us/invent.html

Nevada

Nevada Inventors Association
Reno, NV 89510
Tel: 775 324 3524
E-mail: info@nevadainventors.org
Web: www.nevadainventors.org

Inventors Society of Southern Nevada
Las Vegas, NV 89121
Tel: 702 435 7741
E-mail: Inventssn@aol.com

New Hampshire

New Hampshire Inventors Association
Franklin, NH 03235
Tel: 603 934 1938
Tel: 603 228 3854
E-mail: nhinventors.@yahoo.com

New Jersey

Jersey Shore Inventors

Howell, NJ 07731
Tel: 732 407 8885
Web: ideasbiz@aol.com

Kean University Small Business
Development Center
Union, NJ 07083
Tel: 908 737 4220
E-mail: mkostak@kean.edu
Web: www.njsbdc.com

National Society of Inventors
Cranbury, NJ 08512
Tel: 609 799 4574
Web: www.NationalInventors.com
New Jersey Entrepreneurs Forum
Westfield, NJ 07091
Tel: 908 789 3424
E-mail: contact@njef.org
Web: www.njef.org

New Mexico

Festival of Discovery, Invention and Innovation
Los Alamos, NM 87545
Tel: 505 661 4886
Web: www.nextbigideaLA.com

New Mexico Inventors Club

Albuquerque, NM 87190
Tel: 505 266 3541

New York

Inventors Association of Manhattan, Inc.
New York, NY 10007
Web: www.meetup.com/manhattan-inventors

The Aurora club
South Wales, NY 14139
Tel: 716 652 4704

Inventors Alliance of America –
Buffalo Chapter
Tel: 716 842 4561

NY Society of Professional Inventors
Farmingdale, NY 11735
Tel: 516 798 1490
E-mail: dan.weiss.PE@juno.com
Web: www.Geocities.com/nyspi2001

Long Island Forum for Technology, Inc.
Bay Shore, NY 11706
Tel: 631 969 3700
Tel: 631 755 3321

Inventors Alliance of America

Rochester Chapter
Rochester, NY 14616
Tel: 716 225 3750
E-mail: InventNY@aol.com

Inventors Society of Western New York
Fairport, NY 14450
Tel: 585 223 1225
E-mail: edad0987@aol.com
Web: www.inventny.org

Binghamton Inventors Network
Binghamton, NY 13901
Tel: 607 648 4626
E-mail: mvpierson@aol.com

Inventors & Entrepreneurs of Suffolk
County, Inc.
Melville, NY 11747
Tel: 631 415 5013
Web: www.iesuffolk.com

North Carolina

Inventors' Network of the Carolinas
Charlotte, NC 28202
Tel: 803 242 0556
E-mail: chipcelley@msn.com

North Dakota

Northern Plains Inventors Congress
Bismark, ND
Tel: 800 281 7009
E-mail: info@neustel.com

North Dakota Inventors Congress
Fargo, ND 58103
Tel: 800 281 7009
Tel: 701 252 4959
Web: www.ndinventors.com

Ohio

Inventors Network of Greater Akron
Twinsburgh, OH 44087
Tel: 330 425 1749

Inventor's Council of Cincinnati
Cincinnati, OH 45242
Tel: 513 898 2110
E-mail: Inventorscouncil@inventcincy.org
Web: www.inventcincy.org
Inventors Connection Greater Cleveland
Brunswick, OH 44212
Tel: 330 273 5381
Web: members.aol.com/icgc/index.htm

Inventors Network, Inc.
Columbus, OH 43212
Tel: 614 470 0144
E-mail: 13832667@msn.com

Inventors Council of Canton
Canton, OH 44720
Tel: 330 499 1262
E-mail: FFleischer@neo.rr.com
Web: www.cantoninventorsassociation.org

Inventors Council of Dayton
Dayton, OH 45409
Tel: 937 256 9698
E-mail: swfday@aol.com
Web: www.daytoninventors.com

Youngstown-Warren Inventors Association
Youngstown, OH 44501
Tel: 330 744 4481
E-mail: rjh@mm-lawyers.com
Web: www.3dvirtualmall.com/invwell.htm

Oklahoma

Oklahoma Inventors Congress
Edmond, OK 73083
Tel: 405 348 7794
E-mail: inventor@telepath.com
Web: www.oklahomainventors.com

Weekend Entrepreneurs
Tulsa, OK 74137
Tel: 918 664 5831

Oregon

MicroEnterprise Inventors Program of Oregon
Portland, OR 97202
Tel: 503 998 9560
Web: www.mipooregon.org

Portland Inventors Group
Tel: 503 288 4558
Web: www.portlandinventorsgroup.com

South Oregon Inventors Council
Medford, OR 97501
Tel: 541 772 3478
Lori Capps
North Bend, OR 97450
Tel: 541 756 6866
E-mail: loribdc@uci.net

Blue Mountain Community College
Inventors Group
Pendleton, OR 97801
Tel: 541 276 6233
Web: www.bizcenter.org

Inventors Group at Umpqua Community
College SBDC
Roseburg, Or 97470
Tel: 541 673 8309

Pennsylvania

American Society of Inventors
Philadelphia, PA 19102
Tel: 215 546 6601
E-mail: info@asoi.org
Web: www.asoi.org

Central Pennsylvania Inventors Association
Camp Hill, PA 17011
Tel: 717 763 5742

Pennsylvania Inventors Association
Erie, PA 16510
Tel: 814 825 5820
Web: www.painventors.org

Puerto Rico

Associacion de Inventores de Puerto Rico
San Juan, PR 00918
Tel: 787 518 8570
E-mail: inventorespr@yahoo.com
Web: www.inventorespr.com

South Carolina

Carolina Inventors Council
Taylors, SC 29687
Tel: 864 268 9892
Tel: 864 859 0066

Inventors & Entrepreneurs Association of SC
Greenville, SC 29608
Tel: 864 244 1045

South Dakota

South Dakota Inventors Congress
Brookings, SD 57007
Tel: 605 688 4184

Tennessee

Tennessee Inventors Association
Knoxville, TN 37939
Tel: 865 483 0151
E-mail: jlmins@bellsouth.net
Web: www.tninventors.org

Inventors' Association of Middle Tennessee
Springfield, TN 37172
Tel: 615 681 6462
E-mail: inventorsassociation@hotmail.com
Web: www.iamt.us

Mid South Inventors Association
Collierville, TN 38017
Tel: 901 850 7324
E-mail: Murdock@legacytransfers.com

Texas

Alamo Inventors
San Antonio, TX 78263
Tel: 210 649 2080
Web: www.alamoinventors.org

Amarillo Inventors Association
Amarillo, TX 79109
Tel: 806 367 8610
E-mail: info@amarilloinventors.org
Web: www.amarilloinventors.org

Austin Inventors & Entrepreneurs Association
E-mail: info@austininventors.org
Web: www.austininventors.org
Houston Inventors Association
Houston, TX 77018
Tel: 713 686 7676
Tel: 713 523 3923
E-mail: kenroddy@nol.net
Web: www.inventors.org

Laredo Inventors Association
Laredo, TX 78041
Tel: 956 725 5863

Texas Inventors' Association
Allen, TX 75002
E-mail: wisepatents@yahoo.com
Web: www.txinventors.com

Utah

Utah Inventors
Sandy, UT 84070
Tel: 801 748 1939
E-mail: Osborne@tnw.com
Web: www.utahinventor.org

University of Utah Engineering
Experiment Station
Salt Lake City, UT 84112
Tel: 801 581 6348

Vermont

Invent Vermont
Burlington, VT 05406
Tel: 802 879 7411
E-mail: www.inventvermont.com/contact.php
Web: www.inventvermont.com

Inventors Network of Vermont
Springfield, VT 05156
Tel: 802 885 5100
Tel: 802 885 8178

Virginia

Blue Ridge Inventor's Club
Charlottesville, VA 22906
Tel: 434 973 3708
Tel: 804 973 3708
Web: www.inventorclub.org

Inventors Network of the Capital Area
Annandale, VA 22003
Tel: 703 203 2710
Web: www.dcinventors.org

Virginia Inventors Forum
Williamsburg, VA 23188
Tel: 757 253 5729
E-mail: admin@virginiainventors.org
Web: www.virginiainventors.org

Washington

Whidbey Island Inventor Network
Langley, WA 98260
Tel: 360 678 0269

Inventors Network Vancouver, WA 98668
Tel: 503 239 8299
Tri-Cities Enterprise Association
Richland, WA 99352
Tel: 509 375 3268

Wisconsin

Inventors Network of Wisconsin
Green Bay, WI 54304
Tel: 920 429 0331
Web: www.inventors-network.org

University of WI-Stout Menomonie, WI 54751
Tel: 715 232 5041
E-mail: flyd@uwstout.edu
Twin Ports Inventors & Entrepreneurs Club
Superior, WI 54880
Tel: 715 394 8408
Web: www.lakesuperiorstartups.com

Innovative Minds of Wisconsin
Mosinee, WI 54455
Tel: 715 693 3235

Canada

Inventors Alliance of Canada
Toronto, Ontario M6R 2R6
Tel: 416 410 7792
E-mail: ellwood@netcom.ca

Web: www.inventorsalliance.com

British Columbia Inventors' Society
Vancouver, BC V5N 5W1
Tel: 604 707 0250
Web: www.bcinventor.com

Durham East Independent Inventors' Group
Pickering, Ontario
Tel: 905 686 7172
E-mail: gc7591@hotmail.com

Inventors Club of Brantford
Brantford, Ontario N3T 3W8
Tel: 519 753 7735
E-mail: grahamschram@hotmail.com

Saskatchewan Research Council
Saskatoon, Saskatchewan S7N 2X8
Tel: 306 933 5400
Women's Inventor's Project- Toronto
Thornhill, Ontario L3T 5J4
Tel: 905 731 9691
Web: www.interlog.com/~womenip

Waterloo-Wellington Inventors Club
Cambridge, Ontario
Tel: 519 653 8848
E-mail: svandyk@bserv.com